THE
ARC
OF
LOVE

An Anthology of Lesbian Love Poems

Edited with an Introduction by **Clare Coss**

SCRIBNER

New York London Toronto Sydney Tokyo Singapore

SCRIBNER
1230 Avenue of the Americas
New York, NY 10020

Designed by Chris Welch

Manufactured in the United States of America

1 3 5 7 9 10 8 6 4 2

Library of Congress Cataloging-in-Publication Data
The arc of love : an anthology of lesbian love poems / edited with
an introduction by Clare Coss.
p.   cm.
1. Lesbians—Poetry. 2. Love poetry, American—Woman authors.
3. Lesbians' writings, American. I. Coss, Clare.
PS595.L46A28   1996
811.008'3054—dc20   95-30072
CIP

ISBN 0-684-81446-3

Title Page Photograph:
"Melanie Hope and Catherine Saalfield, New York City, 1994" (Ryo Kazami)

FOR BLANCHE

who calls love the healing art

Poetry is, above all, an approach to the truth of feeling . . . A poem invites you to feel. More than that: it invites you to respond. And better than that: a poem invites a total response.

Muriel Rukeyser

Poetry is the way we help give names to the nameless so it can be thought. The farthest horizons of our hopes and fears are cobbled by our poems, carved from the rock experiences of our daily lives.

Audre Lorde

SAPPHO

In the spring twilight

The full moon is shining:
Girls take their places
as though around an altar

And their feet move

Rhythmically, as tender
feet of Cretan girls
danced once around an

altar of love, crushing
a circle in the soft
smooth flowering grass

CONTENTS

POEMS

THE LIGHT OF LOVE
Sparks   Brief Encounters   Beginnings

THE ORDER OF LOVE
Directions Unchosen and Chosen

SAPPHO / *Thank you, my dear* 98

15

THE VEXATION OF LOVE
Danger   Hate   Healing

16

THE ENDURANCE/EVOLUTION/ECSTASY OF LOVE
Trust and Haven

18

CONTRIBUTORS
(with page references)

ACKNOWLEDGMENTS

The enthusiasm and support of many participants made this anthology possible. Above all, my appreciation goes to the splendid poets who contributed to *The Arc of Love*. I regret that for reasons of space I could not include more of the fine work that has been and is being written.

Thankful recognition is given to the photographers of individual poets whose portraits here appear with their generous consent; and to Joyce Culver, Ryo Kazami, Bettye Lane, and Margaret Randall, whose photographs were used for the title page and part title images.

I am grateful to Charlotte Sheedy, friend and literary agent, for her generative vision and steady commitment to bring a great diversity of feminist and lesbian works to the fore.

Many thanks to Nan Graham, my editor, for her sparkle, spirit, and discernment as she guided *The Arc of Love* to completion. With warmth and efficiency, editorial assistant Gillian Blake forged a path through the thicket of details and deadlines.

Catherine McKinley, permissions manager, not only gathered the permissions with resourcefulness and persistence, she also recommended poets whose vibrant work was new to me. Her expertise from editing her own anthology, *Afrekete*, enhanced this project.

Thanks to the countrywide network for help in locating poets and searching out new work, including: Gloria Anzaldúa, Mi Ok Song Bruining, Michelle Cliff, Dolphin, Frieda Feen, Kenny Fries, Beatrix Gates, Judy Grahn, Joan Larkin, Susan Levinkind, Elena Martinez, Honor Moore, Joan Nestle, Margaret Randall, Bessie Reyna, Susan Sherman, and Makeda Silvera.

I drew on several important anthologies: Beth Brant, ed., *A Gathering of Spirit: A Collection by North American Indian Women*; Shirley Geok-lin Lim, Mayumi Tsutakawa, and Margarita Donnelly, eds., *The Forbidden Stitch; An Asian-American Woman's Anthology*; Sharon Lim-Hing, ed., *The Very Inside: An Anthology of Writing By Asian and Pacific Islander Lesbian and Bisexual Women*; Wendy Mulford, ed., *Love Poems by Women*; Makeda Silvera, ed., *Piece of my Heart: A Lesbian of Colour Anthology*; and Juanita Ramos, ed., *Compañeras: Latina Lesbians*.

Judith McDaniel, Barbara Deming's literary executor, generously gifted this anthology with previously unpublished poems. Nancy Dean wrote the eloquent biographical entry for Jane Chambers. Among her many acts of friendship during this project, Marge Barton received and delivered faxes, always with stimulating editorial observations.

Many hours were spent combing through the comprehensive poetry and photograph collections at the Lesbian Herstory Archives. I am grateful to the team of dedicated volunteers who staff the archives and make hours of research possible at this national treasure-house.

Feminist, lesbian, and gay bookstores including New York City's A Different Light, the late lamented Judith's Room, and Washington D.C.'s Lambda Rising always rewarded me with exciting new publications.

The women and men in my psychotherapy practice continue to teach me about the complexities and possibilities of our lives, how we are and how we can be with each other in this world.

Red roses to my families: original, extended and chosen; and to wise women Audre Lorde and Joan Ormont for our conversations on love over the years.

Profound gratitude goes to Blanche Wiesen Cook, for her steadfast support and inspiring perspectives along the way. This anthology is deeply informed by our twenty-six-year tour around The Arc of Love.

THE

ARC

OF

LOVE

INTRODUCTION

Lesbians have a lot to say about love. Lesbian poets are flourishing as never before. Their poems of revelation are wrested from the flame and fury, lust and loneliness, despair and joy of daily life. They speak of the complexity of relationships with grace and passion.

For twenty years I have been working as a psychotherapist with women in different stages of love—looking for love, in the first throes of love, wanting more from love, not getting enough love, wrestling with love gone wrong, abusive love, lost love, sworn-off love. I hear about lesbians and love from many voices and vantage points. Each woman is unique; but there are patterns that emerge and reemerge as women find their way to the kind of romantic love they want in their lives.

As an activist and writer blessed to have poets and poetry at the heart of my life, lines frequently come to mind illuminating the emotions that define our struggles and our lives.

> *I see you*
> *weaving pain into garlands*
> *the shape of a noose*
> AUDRE LORDE

> *if you lose your*
> *lover comb hair go here*
> *or there get another*
> JUDY GRAHN

> *you mad enough to drive into an abutment,*
> *me mad enough to open my door and jump;*
> MINNIE BRUCE PRATT

I dreamed you were a poem,
I say, a poem I wanted to show someone . . .
ADRIENNE RICH

transformed at last in each other's eyes.
MURIEL RUKEYSER

And I thought how wonderful it would be to gather together a collection of poems around the arc of love—valentines and bittersweets, tempests and praisesongs.

The Arc of Love features the work of eighty-three mostly contemporary poets. Arranged in four parts, each letter in the word *love* reveals the story.

L   is for The Light of Love: Sparks   Brief Encounters   Beginnings
O   is for The Order of Love: Directions Unchosen and Chosen
V   is for The Vexation of Love: Danger   Hate   Healing
E   is for The Endurance/Evolution/Ecstasy of Love: Trust and
     Haven

This collection may enable women to locate themselves along the arc. The single woman, the woman in a relationship, the woman married to a man, the woman who wants to stay single, the woman who can't stand being alone, may find that these poems offer affirmation. Or they may provide comfort for pain past and present; unfurl the sails to adventurous waters; inspire ways of being that were previously undreamed of, unanticipated.

Editing an anthology is extremely personal. Sappho of Lesbos introduces each section, in tribute to the lasting splendor of her ancient legacy. After two thousand years, *sapphist* and *lesbian*—her name and her homeland—are central to our language, although her work was burned and we have only fragments of her art. The frontispiece, "In the spring twilight," is an invitation to dance under the full moon "around an altar of love."

The poems here appeal to my sensibility, open doors to my own understanding, knowledge, and experience of love. Some poems opened doors that surprised me. I was amazed at first by the explicit sexual directness among many contemporary poets, such as Melinda Goodman:

She pulls out
warm wet

fingers steaming in the cold air
put to my lips

Other poets also give voice to what is so often unspoken. Becky Birtha laments the abandonment of lust:

and the bed
is a wide
no one's land
where we never kiss
each other deep and
long anymore

The delight of flirtation leaps off the page in Marilyn Hacker's poem:

Could I concentrate
on anything but your leg against mine
under the table? It was difficult,
but I impersonated an adult

Readings on the compass of love quiver and turn direction in each woman's hand. Adrienne Rich reflects:

the days will run together and stream into years
as the rivers freeze and burn
and I ask myself and you, which of our visions will claim us
which will we claim

There are exciting, fine poets publishing new poems every day. My only regret is that I could not include all the works I admire.

Several questions determined each selection: Is the poem written by a woman who defines herself as a lesbian? Does the poet mostly reside in the United States? Does she want to be published in an anthology of lesbian love poetry? I sought a strong representation of the many voices, visions, and cultures in our community; diverse and splendid works that touch on as many emotions and situations as I could find. Women of African, Asian, Chicana, European, Latina, Native, and Pacific Island heritage are represented, among others. The spectrum ranges from student poets to seasoned writers, from young women to old women, from women on subsistence wages and welfare to women of comfort, leisure, and privilege. Although the anthology features mostly contemporary poets, the legacy of our recent foremothers is represented by Jane Chambers, Barbara Deming, Audre Lorde, Pat Parker, Muriel Rukeyser, May Sarton, Gertrude Stein, and May Swenson.

My selection process began with beloved poets from my own bookshelves and back copies of such journals as *Azalea, Conditions, Feminary, Sinister Wisdom,* and *13th Moon.* I searched for poets new to me at the Lesbian Herstory Archives, A Different Light Bookstore, Judith's Room Bookstore, and the Forty-second Street New York Public Library. I followed leads. Friends made recommendations. Poems arrived in the mail.

"Is lesbian love so different? Love is love," a lesbian friend declared. Having worked with heterosexual and homosexual individuals and couples in my practice, having been married to a man for twelve years and in a lesbian relationship for twenty-six, I agree there are universalities of love. Most of the dynamics between two women along the arc of love will be totally familiar to heterosexual and bisexual women and men, and to gay men.

Nevertheless, there are particularities for women who love women. "Everybody—loves a lover," the song goes. But that is not true for same-sex lovers who are frequently confronted with hate and violence. Two women running into each other's arms on the street, blissfully in love, kissing, walking off arm in arm do not automatically evoke smiles of approval. Such a public display of affection may instead evoke looks of embarrassment or confusion, voyeuristic hostility, verbal abuse, even physical attack. As a result, some of us choose to live in the closet, fearful that we will be rejected, diminished. Earlier lesbians had a romance with the closet and insisted discretion was merely polite. For others it was a matter of life and death—to avoid mental institutions and lobotomy. Today some lesbian mothers choose to live two lives in order to protect their children or grandchildren. Some professional and working women lead double lives and maintain two wardrobes: pumps, stockings, and skirts for the workplace; boots and pants at home. Increasingly, many young and not-so-young lesbians are open, direct, and bold: in your face.

Still, some of our poets do not want to be represented in a book of lesbian writers. One woman told me she identifies herself as bisexual, not lesbian. Another is concerned about the pain and anguish her grown children feel about her sexual preference. Another is protective of her lover's closet at work. Another chooses to come out by having her work appear here.

We live in a society that hates queers and fears women. We try hard not to compound that hatred and turn it in on ourselves or on our partners. To maintain one's independence and identity is always a challenge in a relationship. Two women may have a hard time finding the right balance between closeness and distance. They may have unrealistic expectations of each other as caretakers/caregivers. They may express only loving feelings and withhold hostility until it erupts like a volcano. They may perpetuate neglect or abusive behavior from their personal histories. They may have lower self-esteem because they are women. Because they may feel they are not entitled to power in the world, they may play out power games on each other.

On the other hand, women loving women may be freer to establish a relationship based on equality: I'm a subject; you're a subject. They may find that acknowledging the gamut of feelings from love to hate is not only acceptable but preferable. They may help each other to take responsibility for their own feelings. They may learn to keep their mouths shut and only tell each other thoughts and feelings and ideas that will strengthen their relationship. They may find that the longer they are together, the more their sex life deepens, or they may agree to be or to become companionate partners and to forego sex. They may learn to enjoy an intimacy that honors autonomy, desire, and communion. The poets here, from The Light of Love to The Endurance/Evolution/Ecstasy of Love, articulate and clarify our context and emotions, our actions, values, and choices.

Before the lesbian and gay civil rights movement, ignited by the Stonewall uprising in 1969, poets wrote differently about love. The woman-to-woman encoded poems of Gertrude Stein, Amy Lowell, Edna St. Vincent Millay, H.D., Emily Dickinson, and Elinor Wylie were tantalizing mysteries. But they helped to sustain me as I crossed from a heterosexual marriage "into the life."

That was a long time ago. That was so long ago we used to speculate, do you think Gertrude and Alice are gay? No. Probably not. But they might be. Yes. Maybe they are. . . .

In 1969 my friend Audre Lorde handed me a typescript of a poem, an incredibly bold poem that dared to name the forbidden, to use the language of two women making love.

Out of my flesh that hungers
and my mouth that knows
comes the shape I am seeking

for reason.
The curve of your waiting body
fits my waiting hand
your breasts warm as sunlight
your lips quick as young birds
between your thighs the sweet
*sharp taste of limes.**

In a flash of lightning, Audre's beautiful imagery, her vivid words blazed in recognition of my own experience. This was certainly far removed from my youth, when mother recited to father Elizabeth Barrett Browning's "How do I love thee, let me count the ways . . . " Or when she took to rhyme with Bobbie Burns, "My love is like a red red rose that's newly born in June, my love is like a melody that's sweetly played in tune." Can Audre really do this and get away with it? Can the door be opened on the most tender and sacred exchanges between women, in this most dangerous and mean-spirited world?

Since those earlier days of codes and closets, lesbian poets have burst forth with a freedom to say exactly what they mean. They speak of creating equal and sustained relationships. Beth Brant writes to her cherished partner, Denise:

This life, this love we have chosen and forged to make lasting and beautiful. To make an entity where each of us is whole.

They also buzz from flower to flower. "She was on my list," writes Melinda Goodman.

Outside established gender roles, lesbian poets are versatile. Linda Smukler whets her appetite with fantasy:

you will tell me exactly what I am   a woman and a girl and that I am
also some young boy who you have taken off his bicycle into the woods

They examine love and hate between women. Avotcja asks:

Is it possible for my scared small hand
To reach all the way from Dahomey to Peking

*Audre Lorde, "On the Night of the Full Moon," *Cables to Rage*, London: Paul Breman, 1973, p. 25. Reprinted in *Undersong*, New York: W. W. Norton, 1992, p. 47.

from Ponce to Chung King
And touch you???

Pat Parker cries out:

> *Bitch!*
> *I want to scream*
> *I hate you*
> *Fuck you for this pain*
> *you used my guts*

Our poets can be chaste or astonishing as they chant of ecstasy and passion, ceremonies of the first kiss, rituals of bondage. They are in the vanguard, our troubadours who fearlessly capture the universality and particularity of love between women.

The Arc of Love dispels many myths. These love poems are profoundly political because they are about the wonderful fullness of our complex lives. Women who are lesbian who write poetry: break taboos, hurl aside barriers, do the dishes, live with disability, fight for custody of their children, survive abuse and battering, pay the bills, try to pay the bills, struggle against racism, build nests, endure prison, drink too much, fight too much, withdraw too much, are celibate, enjoy sex, don't enjoy sex.

Lesbian poets write about many subjects, not just love and relationships. Many are fiercely political in the cause of justice for all people. They are angry and activist. They care about dignity; they envision a world of liberty, possibility, and decency. These poems on love are selected out of bodies of work that encompass "root and all, all in all," to quote Tennyson's "Fragment," the first poem I memorized as a child. In that poem a "flower in a crannied nook" is used to celebrate the abundant life that can grow out of stone, given the slightest opportunity, despite the harshest adversity.

Our poets create their lives, give free rein to their imaginations, decipher experience and feeling, and lay their findings out before us. Their work offers steady companionship. *The Arc of Love* is a journey infused with everyday knowledge, erotic passion, spiritual inspiration.

THE
LIGHT
OF
LOVE

"Ain't No Stoppin' Us Now," Gay Rights March, New York City, 1979
(Bettye Lane)

SPARKS
BRIEF ENCOUNTERS
BEGINNINGS

We all want and need love in our lives. Whether we are with partners or single, living with our children or our parents, relatives,
or friends, we seek authentic and enduring love.

Audre Lorde's "Woman" casts a radiant light around the arc of love.
In this woman-loving hymn she demonstrates one aspect of "the power
of the erotic,"* the great respect and appreciation women can have for
each other in this world.

> *I dream of a place between your breasts*
> *to build my house like a haven*

Sparks are those sexual fireworks that explode with great beauty or dazzling intensity against the night sky, and fall to earth quickly. Pamela
Sneed has no regrets.

> *She never stayed*
> *long enough to love*
> *only enough to ignite*
> . . . .
> *she was a bad butch*

For some, lust has a life of its own. A fevered pitch can flare up suddenly between two good friends, as in Fran Winant's bedtime story.

> *"There was a lot of seduction*
> *in that dinner," you laughed.*

*See Audre Lorde's essay, "Uses of the Erotic: The Erotic as Power," *Sister Outsider*,
Trumansburg, N.Y.: Crossing Press, 1984.

35

> *"I was brought up*
> *to take dares," I said.*

Lust keeps moving on.

Brief encounters carry hope and expectations. Is this going to lead to something, or be short-lived and lovely or short-lived and painful? In "How To Have And End An Affair," Jacquie Bishop hesitates on the edge of stanza thirteen:

> *She cares about you*
> *You think about a future realize there's none*
> *wonder why not*

Will this date be worth it? Should I go out with her and see what happens? She certainly appeals to me, or she's not exactly my type, but . . . Melanie Hope takes a chance in "The Day Muni Walked In" with her

> *Tail high dreads swinging from side to side*
> *. . . . .*
> *She caught me lookin' so I winked to gamble it all*

Anita Skeen has us overhear two lovers in a diner's booth having breakfast.

> *in the middle of my scrambled eggs,*
> *you ask the question*
> *I have been thinking for days:*
> How are you feeling
> about this relationship as it now stands?

When a brief encounter works out, and a new relationship is beginning, everything is beautiful, or on its way to becoming beautiful. Two people lose themselves to each other. Time is suspended. There is harmony and seeming equality. In "dinosaurs and larger issues" Irena Klepfisz reaches a point:

> *we know our bodies   and do not mind*
> *them/ourselves   losing all sense*
> *of proportions   limits.   we are equal*
> *here   you and i.*

Susan Sherman sings out:

there is nothing on this earth
more concrete
   than this feeling
I have
  now

for you

Wild and unleashed passion tosses and turns in Magali Alabau's turbulent sexual encounter between Medusa and Clytemnestra. The violent symbolism sweeps them along until

Two women vibrate, mold to each other
die in an embrace
and there are no more wounds, no craters.

In the interest of sex, equilibrium, and bliss, all complaints, irritations, disagreements are suspended for as long as possible. Eventually these must be faced, because love depends on a strong sense of self and appreciation for one's own worth.

SAPPHO

Without warning

As a whirlwind
swoops on an oak
Love shakes my heart

AUDRE LORDE
Woman

I dream of a place between your breasts
to build my house like a haven
where I plant crops
in your body
an endless harvest
where the commonest rock
is moonstone and ebony opal
giving milk to all of my hungers
and your night comes down upon me
like a nurturing rain.

RACHEL GUIDO DEVRIES
Wild

late at night a bird croons. Next door
the neighbor bangs into dark. I lay
alone watching stars appear and dream
of love again, its soft center, my desire

always fills the air with madness
especially in spring at midnight.

The iris begins its urgent press against
the bedroom's wall. The sound of love

is rushing in the creek. Out back
my old dog's spirit calls for a stroll,
stars keep appearing, brighter and brighter,
almost harsh with their gleaming, and you

my secret, only a dream, are wild
and sparkle where the minnows run,
flushed by the moon. I swim and swim
all night, in dark and silky water.

ANA BANTIGUE FAJARDO
Island Dream

Long ago before the whites came
you watched me
from afar
as I paddled my *banca*
up on to the shore
returning from a fishing trip.
You noticed the way
my muscles
tightened
as I drove my paddle
gently through
the ocean waters.
My brown skin
perfectly baked from
the tropical sun,
my rich black hair
dripping with sea water
and sweat—
You noticed the
intensity of my Pinay—

Pilipina eyes—
the way I was one with
my canoe
    with my paddle
    with our mother sea
You waited for me
to ride the wave in,
and you watched as
I slipped my *sarong* off
and lay on the sand
to rest.
You noticed the way
my breasts were
flawlessly molded—
Parang Mayon Volcano,
ang inisip mo. Kay ganda.
How beautiful—you thought.
It was then you could wait no longer
so you approached me.
Malacas na babae, kailangan ko kita.
Strong woman, I need you.

JOAN LARKIN

In the Duchess
SHERIDAN SQUARE, 1971

Women swayed together
on a packed square of scuffed
floor. I stared at the strong

beauty who shook the tambourine,
the poised girl pouring short
pale drinks, the women

whose hips—ample, thin,
pressed close and apart—
cast waves of fire.

I drank their half-closed
eyes, half-opened lips,
link-bracelets, ease

of illegal dancing. Soon
I'd cut my hair, soon
sharpen cuffs and creases,

burn bold as the stone
butch staring back
in whose smile my fear

and wanting found a mirror.
There, amid booze, smoke,
loud unmerciful music,

my whole body was praying
that soon my real life—
dazzling animal whose soft

pelt shone like a woman's
skin—would come
touch me, and at last, I'd dance.

MICHELLE PARKERSON

Conversation With A Missing Person
FOR MARIE

Do you see me, Mother?

    down here tryin' to make my way
    With full moon and girls

Do you catch how we live

    for the pleasure of it?
    Black Heel and Red Stocking

goin' to the dance
      with each other
   Will kiss several times
   before Night is through

   Do you watch your girlchild's passion?

   (The tussle and gleam of it)
   as I learn
   to walk the lines.

E. J. GRAFF

I Met Her At The Bar / 1983

Oh her battered leather jacket, oh her throat's cool curve,
oh did I believe in her sunglasses' twin mirrors?
Did I believe in her bruised and narrow wrists?
Did I believe in her palm against my hip that afternoon

as it wavered in the muck and slag of Central Square,
bums propped against the storefronts, papers slapping hot asphalt,
as ahead of us a dog limped and gnawed its red bandana,
her apartment door unlocked and I

walked in? Don't say the kiss was ruined
by her neighbor's teenage drums. Don't say I wasn't ready
for her sudden hands, her grunts. Don't say
I lay there startled by the dust motes in the sun, the broken
chair beside me on the rug.

GERRY GOMEZ PEARLBERG
First Date With The D.J.

We were in Brooklyn.
Her hand was on my thigh
when we pulled up to the stop sign.
The boys on the corner shouted
"Bulldykes!" and in a flash
she pulled a gun
from her glove compartment
and waved it like a hand-puppet
till they were history.
"They need to know we're armed and dangerous," she said.

We pulled up to my house.
There was a ruby slipper between my thighs,
a poppy field in the back of my brain
though Kansas might as well have been a globe away.
By the time she pulled my sweater off
under the street lamp
and kissed me in that glow,
I could barely remember
the name those kids had called us,
what a gun was, or how to speak
the language we'd been speaking
all our lives.

BEATRIX GATES

From Triptych
II. Cathy

Well, since I became a lesbian . . .
You mean last week, Lynnsey
interrupts laughing. We all
laugh, glad to, after Charlie's

funeral, laughing at how much is
possible after all. Cathy
leaps ahead headlong, Yeah, well,
it's been three weeks, actually.
I'll tell you my life has really
changed. Being HIV Positive
is nothing compared to this.
Course I can't stop talking
about it and you know, not
everyone wants to hear about it either.
This gets a big laugh from back and front
seat. And you people, well my God,
I've got four dykes
right here in one car.
I have to hear all
about how you met, you know,
how you got together.
I don't know what I'm doing.
I've been talking
about it in my meetings
but they think they've heard enough,
what with me being HIV Positive
and all, they don't want to hear
about my being a lesbian too.
They've been through Harry,
my ex-lover dying from AIDS, two
years now it's been, and my ex-
husband and his being positive
now too. You just don't know.
Now my ex-husband, he's
great about my being a lesbian. He's not
threatened or anything. And my support
group in Bangor, they're good,
and of course, the gay/lesbian meeting, but
I need to talk about this a lot
and my regular AA home group
in Bangor, well, one of them,
I thought she was my friend, she says
to me, Cathy, it's too much. We're just
here to talk about problems of alcoholism.

We heard all about Harry's IV drug use
and your HIV, but this is too much.
They think it's a tragedy. She doesn't
understand that I'm happier
than I've ever been in my whole entire
life. After thirty-two years, I am finally
in the right place at the right time.
I'm fine. I don't want to drink. Another thing,
a lot of straight people, they think
if I've said it out loud
once, I should be done.
They don't understand this being
a lesbian changes everything in my life.
Everything. I barely know
what to say anymore, I want
to tell my family and my old
friends from school but I can
see from the reaction
that I'm going to have to be more
selective, pick and choose who
I talk to because I don't need
any shit about this—like I said,
this is the best thing that ever
happened to me. And it *is* related
to my sobriety, goddammit. If I wasn't
sober, I wouldn't know how to think
over anything. I was hiding
in booze, drowning.
Now I'm making some real
choices and I'm pleased as punch
about it. I listen to everyone
else tell about their relationships—
wives, weddings, bosses, you name it.
I don't complain. I get something
out of it. Well, they should
be able to, too. They haven't
heard near enough from me. Why
shouldn't I be able to talk
about being lesbian?
It's good for 'em

to see there are other ways
of loving. My ex-husband,
he understands no problem.
He called in the middle of the night,
the other night. He was freaking out—
not about me—about being positive
now too—and he couldn't think of anyone
else to call. What guy can he call?
Guys don't talk to guys, at least not straight
ones. He doesn't have any supports yet, it's so new.
He kept apologizing for calling
but he really didn't know
who else to call. So I talked with him
for awhile, calmed him down
some, told him it was a big
adjustment and he didn't have to
do it alone, that there were
all kinds of supports now—thanks
to you Lynnsey and you Tracy.
I told him how 2 lesbians started
Downeast AIDS Network and got the guys,
the political ones, working too,
and how you worked with the state
agencies and got grants, how you
started it all in your own home,
had the office on the stairs
and how D.E.A.N. had a big office now
and two paid positions, all because
you just fucking did it, organized
it right here in downeast Maine.
I told him how it was for lovers
and family members, for straight
people too. I gave him
the whole nine yards. I told him he can go
to the support group like I did—
get mad, talk about it,
and eventually he'd maybe get to where
he could accept it and get on
with his life. You know being positive
makes you think. I didn't paint too rosy

a picture for him. The anger, grief,
pain—they all come back. After all
we're only human. But he can
find people, good ones
he can trust, then
get on with it, the way
I have. Anyway, he said he felt
a lot better and thanked me
and said "God bless 'em" about
you Lynnsey and you Tracy.
He'll be all right. I know
he will. But I got to meet
some women. I need to hear
all I can to get ready.
Now Lynnsey and Tracy, you met here in Maine,
right? So there's hope for me.
I need to hear all about it, everything.
Then we can move on to you Bea
and you Roz. You're from another
country. I'd like to hear about that.
Hell, maybe I should come down
to New York and meet some women.

ELENA GEORGIOU

Mooning

Spring—weather's warmer
'Back to Life'—soul to soul
pumps out of open car windows
with the bass turned up so loud
it makes my breast bone vibrate
right down to my stomach churning
last week when i had lunch with her

Falafels on my plate
i didn't eat—couldn't

keep my eyes off her face
thought i saw
a silver hair
in her lashes
like a moon
in a black sky

Saw her nose
for the first time
would look nice pierced
imagined her
with pierced nose
and no clothes
her body moving slowly
making love
lying sideways
at first pressed up close
so our bellies rubbed

Hoped she had a round belly
taking it in turns
to slide on top
with a slow spiralling
motion with mouths
sucking hands cradling
and fingers circling

Leaning across the table
to kiss her goodbye
i hear a warm sound
coming from her chest
and i want white
flowers floating
in a honey bath
and a few seconds stillness
to trace the outline of her lips
with my tongue before i slip it
into her mouth

FRAN WINANT
The Grand Seduction

It was just a day ago
at about this time,
I was sitting here feeling sleepy
though it was only a quarter of nine
and I thought I'd call you to say,
"Come over tomorrow night
and share with me the birthday dinner
I made for someone
who didn't seem to have the time."

When you answered the phone you said,
"Well, isn't this a big surprise?
I'm sitting here with a $5 steak
a woman turned down tonight.
She was in a sick and angry mood,
had her period besides.
I'd made plans to seduce her,
she went home
and left me a bouquet of flowers.

So let's have dinner tonight,
you bring yours and I'll broil mine.
We'll sit in the *Salon des Refusès*
drinking my red wine.
We'll laugh away our losses,
toast our future success,
and tell the tale of the Grand Seduction
that might have been
but just didn't happen this time."

Your steak was medium rare,
it had the look and taste of flesh,
but to my surprise, I didn't mind.
It went well with your red wine.
"I don't know why I wanted her anyway.
She bored me," you said.
"Guess I thought it would be easy

to share with a stranger
what I wouldn't
dare with a friend."

Your salad had a special nutmeg dressing
that made it taste like dessert,
and my eggplant parmesan birthday dinner
was so bittersweet it almost hurt.
"This is fun," I said.
"This is the way it should be—
Sharing with a friend the best we offer.
There isn't anyone
who deserves it more."

Our conversation wasn't boring,
it was full of our life and concerns.
We were giving names to your paintings
so they could go out into the world.
Between "Blue Sage" and "Purple Passion,"
your hand reached out to my breast.
"There was a lot of seduction
    in that dinner," you laughed.
"I was brought up
to take dares," I said.

"Well, there's the door to the
    bedroom," you said.
"Who'll be the first to go through?
I don't seem to be moving
and neither do you."
So we went through the door together
and lay down in a dream.
"This is just play, it's just a game,"
    you said.
"We'll hold each other for a while,
then you'll leave."

You said I was going to be trouble,
you frowned and shook your head.
Then our clothes were gone

and our bodies answered
the songs that slept in the bed.
I reached up for your face,
it was softer than I'd guessed,
and in your mouth I drowned forever,
like the steak,
the red wine, and the salad greens.

"Why are you holding me?" you said.
"What is it that you need?"
"Do you want something from me?" you said.
"Is that why you're holding me?"
"I just want to hold you," I said,
"rest my face on your breasts,
sense the force of our intense bodies,
be blessed
by the grace that moves in our flesh."

All through work the next day
I couldn't wait to get home to the phone
to tell you about the vibration inside me
that felt almost as good as love.
"Why are you calling me?" you said.
"Don't ask for another time
when we laugh and feast
    and share our pleasure.
The Grand Seduction
was only meant for one night."

EILEEN MYLES

Warrior

Sensation of the supermarket
I can go this far
you're curling & wild
almost dying in the car ten seconds

out of water, you don't travel
well. Your smell is not sweet
but itchy, like sex in the woods
rarely does one purchase
such a smell. Usually stumbled
on, remembered. So while you're almost
vanishing, I'll say we were spontaneous
How did such white meet such fuschia
& then hot pink. A smattering
of intelligent antennae
a scribble of brains
amidst the curly blossoms
and the thin slim pods
future flowers, it's clear
you've got a way to go. Anyone can
look at you real fast & say
she's everything. I see cactus,
I feel thorny prickles, no one
knew your name, no one in the fruit
stand at 9 & 9G. & I rode home
with your flavors on my lap.
& I say this for wildness
even as it's dying
it's very very powerful

MELINDA GOODMAN
New Comers

Saturday:

Nobody trusts CD cause she
plays like she's in love
when all she wants
is to fuck.

She gives me a big juicy hug
when I walk in the meeting.
Rubbing her breasts all on mine. I can barely see her
through my shades that are too dark but go
with the outfit. Kissing me on the mouth, she grrrrs
in the back of her throat like some imitation
tiger woman.
I smile
and get away from her.

Monday:

Here I am at another meeting.
CD's there on a bench.
Nothing but men here today.
I feel like leaving.
Then CD spots me . . . motions . . . come sit next to her.
I go over. Feel the heat of her arm
pushing against the side of mine.
We're supposed to be listening
to what these guys are talking about
but all I know is CD's thigh
against the side of *my* thigh.
Then she says in a low voice,
"Come."

We go to the crumbling
church basement bathroom.
I feel her belt buckle that says CD in brass
as she pushes me through the stall door
kisses my back
unsnaps my jeans
rubs hard through the seams of my Wranglers
going in layered stages
like I can stop her any time
teasing my clit
like a diamond earlobe
tightening my nipples
I lick her lips

unbuckle her belt
she spins me toward the stall wall
pulls down my pants and plunges
up to my eyeballs
with nicotine fingers

Bending my knees to take her deeper
I reach back to feel her bigger
hips pushing against me
cheekbones rub
graffitied metal
fingers
stiffening inside
as I come
quiet
resting
leaning against her
catching my breath

She pulls out
warm wet
fingers steaming in the cold air
put to my lips
to be sucked clean
fucking my mouth
til I can't taste me anymore

I pull up my jeans
tuck in my blouse
she unlatches the door
whispers some bullshit
about what a hot mama I am
then we leave

she can't wait to tell her friends
she got me
I don't care
she was
on my list.

PAMELA SNEED
Languages I Never Learned

She collected women like trophies
assorted shapes and sizes
colors and contours
each affirmed her ability
to make even modest women
want to climb inside her skin
like soldiers seeking refuge
from the storm.

She never stayed
long enough to love
only enough to ignite
their attention
but when they began
to clear their closets
she talked of travelling
and needing a larger space.

I knew I never should have
gotten involved with that woman
I knew I never should have
gotten involved with that woman
part of her power being
she was a bad butch
who made women unravel

come undone at the seams
like wonder woman
beneath her armor
was desperate
I knew I never should have
gotten involved with that woman

but somewhere inside
she moved me
to another country
and I started speaking
languages I'd never learned.

JACQUIE BISHOP
How To Have And End An Affair
FOR BIRDLADY AND MICHAEL LASSELL

1. Bump into each other on a Monday
   notice it's been awhile since you last saw each other
   laugh, kiss hello, promise to talk
   take your seat on opposite ends of the auditorium
   the show's starting
   Think: She's cuter than before
   Watch who She is with
   wonder about the relationship
   Turn your attention to the stage

2. Days later ask a friend for Her number
   Call   wait for the beep
   say "hello" "call when you can" "nothing important"
   Call back   wait for the beep
   leave Her your number
   Wait

3. Speak with your best girlfriend
   talk about your "ex-"
   notice what you feel
   then talk about Her
   wonder if She flirted
   question if She was just being friendly
   Remember the broadness of Her smile
   know   she flirted with you
   Wait

4. Jump when the phone rings
   Act casual when you realize it's Her
   Notice Her voice is higher than you prefer
   Find things you don't like
   Giggle (you never giggle)
   wonder about Her tongue
   smile

5. Ask about Her lover they broke up
   tell Her about yours you broke up
   be silent for a moment

6. It's your birthday
   you're doing different things
   calling Her was one
   She's glad you called
   2 ½ hours later She asks you out
   accept without hesitation
   ½ hour more you hang-up

7. Call your best friend back
   giggle   give her the good news
   thank her for support   hug over the phone

8. Speak of your "ex-"
   notice your voice is soft and low
   answer the call waiting
   it's Her again
   say good-bye to your friend
   she understands
   smile   touch yourself
   talk for another hour

9. Get dressed three   four times
   settle on something lacey and black and red
   give a message
   then doubt yourself
   feel

10. See each other 2 sometimes 3 times a week
    fuck on the bed
    the floor
    in the kitchen and bathroom
    for awhile
    never go out together
    or eat together
    or piss with the door open

11. Think about your "ex-"
    lie in another woman's arms
    smile when She is looking
    fuck   make love   care more than you should
    don't tell Her it still hurts
    that's what friends are for
    kiss hard
    cry inside
    ask Her to hold you
    wonder if She can tell
    hope that She can   can't

12. Ask for more
    go dancing   to movies   to dinner
    Share stories about childhood and lovers
    and work and family
    Speak everyday except when there are others
    It's more than a fling
    People ask if She's your lover
    you become nervous with its meaning
    but you like the way it sounds
    then watch as She blushes when asked the same
    wonder what She feels   ask   then blank out the answer

13. She cares about you
    You think about a future realize there's none
    wonder why not

14. Call your "ex-"
    Sleep with her
    Make love to her
    Make promises
    Know that you can't have them both
    Choose one   Choose your "ex-"   feel
    guilt and love and anger and loss
    Choose your "ex-"
    you never wanted to break-up or move or cry
    Choose her because she apologized
    You still love her

15. Recognize you love Her
    confess it was something more   than just an affair
    Feel it   fear it
    then smile and eat and laugh and cry
    make love and promises
    But tell Her good-bye

ELIZABETH LORDE-ROLLINS

The Wedding of the Woman in the Closet

"I'm in love with him," you said
looking very secure in the fact
confusion had a party in my head
you maintained what came before was just an act.
Maybe this lie will keep you safe from where I go.
My dear, you really put on quite a show.

A marriage for Daddy's Little Girl
(daddy's gone, now she's thirty-two)
How perfect! Frills, eyeshadow and curl
but I'd look again if I were you.
Make the bed before you go,
Sweetheart—you put on quite a show.

And, Love, I couldn't help but remember your lips
so sweet and soft; likewise your bedroom smile
your swaying breasts, your silky hips
more than I *ever* imagined, quite shattered by your style.
Oh! All that hair loosened and your eyes all aglow
No wonder it's hard to believe your new show.

Not that you were easy. We were a game I played hard
I never let you rest, I admit
Pianissimo, then fortissimo, crescendo, ritard;
but face it, dear, you appreciated more than my wit.
I can hear you still: "Not so fast—mm, but not too slow"
I had great seats to see it. Was that too a show?

Steadily staring at the women, you could pick out all the signs
concluding "Lesbians don't have their nails done
and they are never perfect nines."
At request, your mother painted yours one by one.
I've known you too well, but honey, she'll never know
Ten points, Painted Lady, you put on quite a show.

The relatives were ready and the lines were drawn
to my own refrain of "let her go" I stood:
best friend of the bride, ambivalent pawn
with my eyes like rubies and my face of wood.
Your mother perched on her branch and grinned like a crow.
She'd waited ten years for this particular show.

And so you married that gentle knight
I danced with him too—your honorable maid
you, my lover, dressed to leave in white
after all, this is how weddings are played.
Dearest, Spring is ending: may he never be your foe
it will be a cold day in hell
when I catch your next show.

MARDY MURPHY
Sweet Basil—The Greek Suite

#1
Sweet Basil

The Greeks plant it by the blue shuttered doors for good luck
they bring it to the altar and pray; smother its incense with incense
bathe it in olive oil and vinegar
roast with spring lamb

sweet basil moves in my mouth like you do
all pungent, all flavor
tongues are taut for telling

ancient herbs
the meaning of a civilization lost for eons

whether wild-growing like mustard in California fields
or cultivated for an acquired taste they say
rub it on before you swim in the Aegean
you might find old gold and a new lover

MAGALI ALABAU

From Electra, Clytemnestra
TRANSLATED BY ANNE TWITTY

VII

The wind sounds deep.
The Mycenaean sea stifles its hoarse voice,
a volcano dilating.
Medusa walks in the hills,
her serpents swell
and swell.
The dark wall that covers everything
is watching,
wildly cackling.
Medusa raises her hooves and drives them into the earth.
Medusa opens and closes her eyelashes.
Her mouth is a hawser stretching toward war.
She goes to the room
to flood the fortress.
Opens the door
and sways and sways
fury, crater
she bites the furniture, the floor
a shameless panther. Eyes search upwards,
glance to one side
travel everywhere
she sways her back, arching each tier of her crest.

The room a giant fire and on the throne of solitude
Clytemnestra seats herself.
And feels Medusa's tongue on her feet,
on each breast.
Her nipples turn to fountains.
Pleasure enters.
Medusa scrubs her and strips her,
lashes her, shakes her, and holds her up. She mounts on her neck,
muddies her face.
Tongue with tongue,
red, thick foam.
Her lips scald, ears burn.
So many serpents in a clitoris
such strong, thirsty softness.
Faces lick each other; their eyes fixed.
Two wild beasts look at each other
throw themselves into a long bed.
Medusa mounts a long horse
the roof crushes them
and they unite
and they unite
and they love
and they use their teeth, cutting each other.
Medusa enters her mouth, her back, and cries out.
Each serpent inhabits an orifice.
Clytemnestra barks.
Her clasped arms bleed on the great head.
Two women vibrate, mold to each other
die in an embrace
and there are no more wounds, no craters.
Mycenae is reborn.
The sun aims and blazes into a drenched bed.
Ruins of union descend through the doors
a thick cape flowing outward.
Stairs whine and laugh, creaking,
pleasure fells them.
The milk of the two becomes one
and flows down to the sea.
Clytemnestra has given her hard breasts.

Clytemnestra has received hands and hands and flesh
into her mouth.
Her mouth is dry, her waist slim.
In the midst of perfection she turns her head to give the final kiss
of the night
and sees Electra.

MAGALI ALABAU

From Electra, Clitemnestra

VII

El viento suena hondo.
El mar de Micenas acalla su ronquera,   ·
es un volcán en vilo.
Medusa anda en las colinas,
sus serpientes se inflan
y se inflan.
La tapia oscura que todo lo cubre
está mirando,
riendo a carcajadas.
Medusa saca sus pezuñas y las clava en la tierra.
Medusa abre y cierra las pestañas.
Su boca es un cordón ancho hacia la guerra.
Al cuarto va
a inundar la fortaleza.
Abre la puerta
y se menea y se menea
furia, cráter
muerde los muebles, el piso
como una pantera con agallas. Los ojos van arriba,
van de lado
van a todas partes
menea su lomo, su cresta en cada filo.
El cuarto es un fuego gigante y en el trono de soledad

Clitemnestra se sienta.
Y siente la lengua de Medusa en los pies,
en cada seno.
Sus pezones se hacen fuentes.
El placer entra.
Medusa la restriega y la desnuda,
la latiga, la sacude y la alza. Se le monta en el cuello,
le embarra la cara.
Lengua con lengua,
espuma roja, espesa.
Los labios queman, arden las orejas
Tantas serpientes en un clitoris
tanta blandura fuerte, sedienta.
Las caras se lamen; los ojos se encuadran
Las dos fieras se miran
Se tiran en una cama larga
Medusa monta un caballo largo
el techo las aplasta
y se unen
y se unen
y se aman
y se cortan de dientes.
Medusa le entra por la boca, por la espalda, y grita
Cada serpiente ocupa un orificio
Clitemnestra ladra.
Sus brazos amarrados a la gran cabeza desangran.
Dos mujeres vibran, se amoldan
mueren abrazadas
y ya no hay heridas ni cráteres.
Micenas renace.
El sol apunta y clava su fuego en una cama muy mojada.
Ruinas de unión descienden por las puertas
como una capa espesamente caminando hacia afuera.
Las escaleras gimen y rien, crujen,
el placer las desploma.
La leche de las dos se junta en una sola
y baja hacia el mar.
Clitemnestra ha dado sus senos duros
Clitemnestra ha recibido manos y manos y carne
en la boca

Su boca está seca, la cintura delgada.
En medio de la perfección vuelve la cabeza a dar el
último beso de la noche
y ve a Electra.

JUDY GRAHN
I only have one reason for living

I only have one reason for living
and that's you
And if I didn't have you as a
reason for living,
I would think of something else.

AVOTCJA
Afro-Asia

Is it possible to step out of my cowardice
Or to cross the unending forbidden lines
Or to swim the oceans of cultural tabus
Or cross the many continents
That separate us
That have always separated people like us

Is it possible for the Chinese thunder
That has for so long knocked gently at my insides
And run burning its way through my veins
To blend with Afro-Boricua rhythms
What does it sound like . . . . this music???
African/Asian/Native American melodies?
You & I?????
Is it possible to build a bridge from Dahomey to Peking

From Ponce to Chung King
And dance gently back & forth
Always & never disturbing the natural flow of the universe
Can I cross that bridge completely blind
Completely blind with very strong human feelings
In this very inhuman world

Is it possible for my scared small hand
To reach all the way from Dahomey to Peking
from Ponce to Chung King
And touch you???

MELANIE HOPE
The Day Muni Walked In

When Muni walked in she was a knockout
Right on sister girl had my nose real wide
When Muni walked in she was a knockout
Tail high dreads swinging from side to side

I was in my corner chillin' ponderin' my 9-2-5
I was in my corner ponderin' my 9-2-5

She said "How y'all dwine"
Ole Jack she said "Fine"
She said "How y'all dwine"
Ole Jack she said "Fine"

I took a spies long look and another sip o' wine
I took a spies long look and another sip o' wine

Done ran already done ran so many
Don't nobody know which way the numbers will fall
Done ran already done ran so many
Maybe today will be my way the numbers fall

She caught me lookin' so I winked to gamble it all
She caught me starin' and I just gambled it all

Two weeks later I was in my same corner
Muni was next to me we were both sippin' wine
Two weeks later I was sittin' real pretty
With Muni by my side

ELIZABETH CLARE

How To Talk To A New Lover
About Cerebral Palsy

Tell her: *Complete strangers*
have patted my head, kissed
my cheek, called me courageous.

Tell this story more than once, ask
her to hold you, rock you
against her body, breast to back,

her arms curving round, only
you flinch unchosen, right arm trembles.
Don't use the word *spastic.*

> In Europe after centuries
> of death by exposure
> and drowning,
> they banished us
> to the streets.

Let her feel the tension burn down your arms,
tremors jump. Take it slow: when she asks
about the difference between CP and MS,

refrain from handing her an encyclopedia.
If you leave, know that you will ache.
Resist the urge to ignore your body. Tell her:

They taunted me retard, cripple,
defect. The words sank into my body.
The rocks and fists left bruises.

Gimps and crips, caps
in hand, we still
wander the streets but now
the options abound: telethons,
nursing homes, and welfare lines.

Try not to be ashamed as you flinch and tremble
under her warm hands. Think of the stories
you haven't told yet. Tension grips fierce.

Ask her what she thinks as your hands shake
along her body, sleep curled against her,
and remember to listen: she might surprise you.

SUZANNE GARDINIER

Where Blind Sorrow Is Taught To See
Book Four

Before you I walked with my hands in my pockets
by the dark deserted piers in all weathers
Before you I asked at the oracles
of steel grates and park maples' winter cordage
and tried to decipher the admonitions
of saplings and windows of notebooks and globes
Before you I bluffed and hoarded I ranged
the inconsolable archipelago
bent with useless offerings ungiven
past taverns and perfume and cardboard pallets

longing for the embrace of mannequins
trying to walk captivity's scent
from my clothes Before you I could not hold
oblivion tightly enough against me
The parsed days' murders and educations
settled into the bones of my face
where I could no longer understand them
Before you blank tablets Before you dumb
Before you I looked for you in the rubble
of roadways and broken pediments
in the praying mantis climbing the pilaster
in the bleak hacked view from the promontory
in cuffed new leaves stirring in empty shoes
Before you I walked and whistled invitations
and heard no answering voice before you

EILEEN MYLES

At Last

I always fall in love with tired
women. It seems I have the
time. On the blackboard
at the Gay Community
Center it said:
Ladies, we need your
blood. Afterwards
come to the Women's
Coffee House and
have a cup of
coffee. Donation
$1.00. He won't
be complaining
about his big
toe that hurts.
The man who
died last

night. The Death
Squad has taken
him away. I thought
of all the clothes
that guy must've
had. Now no one
can stand to
wear them. I use
Central America
& Southeast
Asia to ease
my mind. Pauline
Kael says that's
squalid. We live
in a culture of
vanishing men.
What is the difference.
Vincent's big joke
is his five-year
membership to
a video club.
They got him on
the phone at the
hospital. He
didn't know
how to say
one year
would probably
do just fine.
Another
thin man does
a night club
act—he does
show tunes
to the horror
of his visiting
friends. He'll
take it on
the road once
he gets better.

At last he knows
what he wants
to do! Jimmy Wayne's
family says Well,
that's what you
get. But I get
something dif-
ferent. What I
do at my desk
is always different
from what I do
on my bed. I was
watching the dif-
ference last
week. This week
I'm different
again. Is it because
of windows that
I think the
day's square
and life is
shaped like
a train. The big
buds outside
my window
make me think
I'm outside
of life because
I can watch
her change
and she can't
see me. You'd
think I'd be
grateful for
my vision. It is
complex. A dance
of images gates
and branches
across buildings
statues windows

firescapes and
creeping cats.
Honey, life
is a blast
and I am
part of it
but you're
separate
from me.
It's how you
want it. The radio
starts up
and I nearly
lose my style.
I opened
my heart to
you and now
I feel like
an open wound.
I put my arms
around you
I thought
you felt
great. I called
it heaven
one day

disturbing
once the
train moved

now nothing's
the same.

LÊ THI DIEM THÚY

Foresee

you said
why does it take so long to be

night time?

i never thought it would take so long
to get dark

and you were waiting for
the kiss
the confession
the surprise
the aching
denial
the aching
desire

say
a fire comes
and
takes us
say
we just didn't know
it would be
like
this
we didn't know it could be

let it be
let it go

you grasp hands full of
sand
let it fall between your toes

if i win the lottery
i will have a house
on skinny legs which
always threatens
to fall
into the ocean
and
it has
a winding staircase
which
falls down
into the ocean
and
every morning
every time
i wake up with you
climbing
with me
down
into the ocean
then

it's night time
coming
dark

like i always knew
it could
be

LINDA SMUKLER
Telephone II

(I was out to dinner and wanted to get up and say to all of them: I am
in love with someone who is not sitting at this table.)
You tell me this over the phone and in the next breath ask me to be a

young man off the street when it's hot and I am sweaty and I have followed you home   I will do anything for you and tell you that I watch you secretly as you bathe and then lotion yourself   put on silk panties and camisole   I will do anything for you and suddenly I grab your arm and drag you into the bedroom   I tell you that you will never do what you have done   that you will never again walk in front of me and tantalize me   I will force open your legs   I will touch your clit and tell you that you are shameful and that you will not be separate from me   that I will take you any moment I want   do you understand?   you ask me over the phone to be a young man off the street and after you come you order me to lie down   I will do anything for you but this is more difficult   OK I say   besides I have to pee and you   a woman   will not let me for hour after hour until it becomes unbearably painful and your voice takes over and you hold my cunt in your hand and you will punish me severely if I can't hold it any longer   you say you will parade me around the bedroom in a dress   that only you will have this and know as I walk around the world in suits and ties and white shirts   you will tell me exactly what I am   a woman and a girl and that I am also some young boy who you have taken off his bicycle into the woods and shown him your cock and played with his little dick   that you show him how to get hard and show him how you get hard and at some time he gets frightened and you turn him over and fuck him in the ass and bring him off with your hand yanking on his dick and now you are some tough ravishing woman who loves me   grime and all   who will tear it all apart for me   one strand at a time   who will put it all back

HONOR MOORE
First Night

I saw clitoris.   You saw tongues.
We knew we would talk through the night
and in darkness stood at the fire
watching heat swell until words
we could not say formed a silence
we would not break.   "I don't want this to

end," I said.   Soon we were foot to
foot at ends of a bed, my tongue
fluttering free of lips that find silence
in such matters easier.   As night
settled,   I watched your face as words
flew from our mouths—stories at a fire—

first loves, deaths of parents.   When the fire
lost heat we carried wood, no heed to
darkness passing.   I was stumbling for words
to perform a task meant for tongues,
but mine was tied, inexorably as night
holds course and dawn brings a silence

between tree-toad and birdsong.   Silence
of repose is one thing; this was fire
compressed.   How long could I swallow?   Night
would end!   We laughed, raised ice cream to
each other, licked spoons clean as tongues
of fire, held breath until certain words

broke fear as rain eases heat, words
gave way to touch, and what had been silence
became cacophony.   Yes, I saw tongues,
embers brighten like labia.   Yes, fire
can take any form you wish it to
when eyes are tempered by the night.

We stoked the fire to burn past the night,
at dawn lay side by side until words—
gathering, cluttering—exhausted us to
feeling and what had speech wanted silence,
until sun burned through mist like fire
through wood and light loosened our tongues.

For night's measure we kept that silence,
but morning brought words to commit its fire
to memory.   *Clitoris* I said.   You said *Tongues*.

MELANIE KAYE/KANTROWITZ

I Tishri/Rosh Hashonah

FOR L.V.

In bed this morning light
comes from two directions:
west, south: bathing the oldest cat in new
sun. I watch the still-green trees on the verge of turn-
ing red, yellow: today begins the different
year, day first in the Jewish world, the name

is Rosh Hashonah for the 5746th time. Love names
my hands over your body and your light
hair brings sun into the room, even at dusk. We're different
but our hungry bodies wake in all directions
twining as the earth turns
making each other new

as our love is new, and the downstairs kittens, and the new
page in my book. My people's history is old, named
before the Book was written, before Moses returned
from Sinai, before Sarah brought Isaac into the light.
My people, scattered in four directions
over the world, each hour meet this day differently

with prayers   songs   memory   indifference—
day for apples and honey—to coat the new
harvest   ample and sweet, directing
us to remember *l'shana tova*—may your name
be inscribed sweetly, as light
moves west over the ocean and Jews turn

to or from the name Jew, turn
to shul or to the bleached indifference
of America where history weighs in light,
less and less, until we are scraped as new
as the bland norm with the shortest name
urging *enter   forget   here is the one direction.*

In bed with you this morning I wonder what directions
Jews take   today; tomorrow; is it our turn
to heal—just a little—nothing to name
with history? Does love, does memory make a difference?
Do I know a song to sing my new
love for the new year's light?

And are my people's directions so different
we share only a name? and what will this new
year turn over into the light?

ADRIENNE RICH

From Twenty-one Love Poems

II

I wake up in your bed. I know I have been dreaming.
Much earlier, the alarm broke us from each other,
you've been at your desk for hours. I know what I dreamed:
our friend the poet comes into my room
where I've been writing for days,
drafts, carbons, poems are scattered everywhere,
and I want to show her one poem
which is the poem of my life. But I hesitate,
and wake. You've kissed my hair
to wake me. *I dreamed you were a poem,*
I say, *a poem I wanted to show someone . . .*
and I laugh and fall dreaming again
of the desire to show you to everyone I love,
to move openly together
in the pull of gravity, which is not simple,
which carries the feathered grass a long way down the upbreathing air.

ANITA SKEEN
Over Breakfast

in the middle of my scrambled eggs,
you ask the question
I have been thinking for days:
How are you feeling
about this relationship as it now stands?
My fork spears a finger
on my left hand as my interest
in hash browns becomes clinical.
All I know how to do is grin
when I look at you,
unwinding your cinnamon roll
like an ace bandage.
You are grinning, too.
Positive, I say
as I feel my body wired
with electric shock, my knife
a chainsaw shredding
the bread. I press potatoes
and eggs into a long soft wall
between us, recalling something
about fences and good neighbors.
Answering questions clearly
is a skill I never learned.
I tried for gymnastics instead.
Can I cartwheel my way through?
I am already tripping the balance beam.
Uneven parallels are next.
In this tiny diner,
already crowded before eight,
the waitress spins
from booth to booth
like a song on the wrong speed.
As she rotates by, you ask
only for more coffee.

GABRIELLE GLANCY
E-Message Moscow

Like some wind in a foreign language
dressed up in your accent pronounced
over and over soundlessly into the air
waves which tremble to the pitch of night
between us *I had a glass of plum wine.*
Just at that moment the connection flickered.
The thought was trivial—I was only mildly
drunk though still intoxicated—in fact, it was
immaterial, if symbolic. The signs like flecks
of colored light were beautiful but impossible
to decipher. Now the pitch is even higher.
From your country the comet hit the face
of Jupiter eleven hours before it hit here
just as I was sitting up in sleep as if in
sudden prayer heart beating like a cursor
as if in answer to the message that flashed
like the thought of touching you across
the screen. The wine was deliciously fortuitous
if you can believe it and like a kiss blown on-line
through light years went straight to my head.
A piece of world bigger than the earth?
As they say in Russian, even the hedgehog
understands as a star trembles through
the night's electric body: I am madly in love.

IRENA KLEPFISZ
dinosaurs and larger issues
FOR RACHEL

i

1. & 2.   the first two nights
she lay   diagonally across

the bed   clutching at the blankets
she refused me   room & warmth

3.   the third night
she told me   i can't handle
this   i can't handle   it
i slept   in the living room

4.   the fourth night
she said   this has to be
the last night   & moved
close to me

5.   the fifth night
she did not speak   about
it.

ii.

they're never as big as i imagine
rachel informs me   whenever i enter
the reptile house   expecting cobras
to be jammed   wedged   bursting out of
into   every corner of the cage   muscles
tensing   i am always disappointed
with their slenderness   their comfort
and ease   as they relax   draping casually
over plastic trees

whales   she is earnest   should
be as big as ocean liners   instead
they swim content   in aquariums
trained to jump and leap   and it's true
they're large   but not like
they're supposed to be

rachel's eyes   narrow and widen
i do not reveal   some dinosaurs
full grown   were no bigger

than hens   that she could have
roasted   and served them
for dinner   with no fear of
leftovers

iii

in the dark   her features
are distinct   her skin white
translucent.   i see outlines
of bones.   she is crystal
my fingers   feel the thinness
of the flesh.   her mouth
is hard   demanding.   she
keeps her head turned away.
she does not look   directly
at me   except to brush away
the hair from my face   before
her tongue penetrates my mouth.
then her eyes close quickly.
i study the hand's gesture
try to give it meaning.

in the dark   her features
are strong.   she lies relaxed
ready to accept   the touch
of my tongue   ready to be cupped
sucked into me   later she says
i cannot reciprocate.

iv

no i don't enjoy this
she says   biting my hand.
her mouth   which holds
endless kisses   will never
say yes to me   just the hand
across my back   like a heavy hammer

or a quick furtive kiss
on the back of my neck
tell me   perhaps   yes.

i just don't like cunts
she says   i don't like
them   she says to me.

v

i am sorry if i've made
you unhappy   i told her
sitting   at the furthest end
of the couch
               don't make
yourself so important
she answered   with confidence
there are larger issues
at stake.

vi

it's not the kind of person
you are   i try to explain to her
you have the power   to lift
your hand   to touch me as i pass
or to walk towards me   and hold
my face   so it's not the kind
of person   you are

vii

at night   the vestiges
of other ages   influence
us.   there are
the sucking sounds   of your mouth
with mine   the moans of an ancient language

i easily recognize   my tongue
urging you on   slowly   deep
beneath the sea   or in some secret
cave   our nails: clawed   we hold
each other   you and i
released from an unexpected
danger.   exhausted we lick
each other's wounds   inflict
new ones   sharply.   our voices
echo   through the cave
return   and clash   on hard rock.

we know our bodies   and do not mind
them/ourselves   losing all sense
of proportions   limits.   we are equal
here   you and i.

afterwards   in the fire's flames
we see   cumbersome dinosaurs
rubbing their necks   against
each other   making small   sweet noises
tame and huge   so much larger than we dared imagine.

PAULA GUNN ALLEN
Arousings

1.

clear the ditch
the roadway.
get them freed and long,
walk alongside them watch
water running
clear and frothy, cold.
let the rain
in through the pores

let it wash clear the pane,
let the air in, break
the glass, stay within the bounds
of reason, loading up with things
lovely and necessary, things
that are dry, things that are lost.
go away from meaning into longing.
go far and long, go wide, go deep, go on.
let the craft go on pitching
on the highhigh waves,
let it cast the winds away, let
the rain go down the face, the trunk,
the body's limbs, let it roar and tumble,
let the wind wash clear
the dire spaces, all disease,
the tall twisted places of the dark,
the roman arches, the goths and visigoths,
the slaughter.
let the water drench with laughter,
with what there is that's cool,
with what there is that's sweet.
at Laguna in the proper season
they clean the ditches.
so life bearer will freely pour.
they call it wonder.
water.
they call it thought.
they call it peaceful hearts
and sharing. caring. caring for.

2.

across the emptiness of grey
spray of rain on the highway
becoming your face,
across the moisture-laden miles
the hills pouring with her sweat
her grateful tears of release,
recognition, recognized

see her, how she rises
her breath frothy deep on the air,
her gasping, her need:
she has a new lover this year.
have you noticed how wet
she's becoming, how erratic?
she smiles and roars,
pours in perfect passion,
tosses her hair, body,
her legs,
she claps her hands, she sings.
she dances.
the grandlady, so fine this year,
this season, this solstice, this
solace, this spring.
and your eyes grey reflect her joy
they glow like miles at sea, like rising
fog. i think of her touch,
your hands
subtle and quick.
i think of small furry creatures, ferret, raccoon.
of how you spit and hissed the first year through,
how you bit me then:
tiny sharp teeth baring
so lately let free from the cage
of mortality. of your fear.
i think of how you loved
desperately.

3.

how you loved me. made love to me.
what i saw there when i was held.
in the wild tangle of our tongues' necessity,
rooting in softleafed places,
melting and pouring like the hills today,
ground gone to water, running toward the sea,
heat rising but not in rage.
in love.

just the seagrey of your gaze,
your longing, arms raised to clasp
me,
    in sight
        of the Woman
   she
      lying in a pond
          in the woods
in the pond of her self,
            her dreams
lying breathless, she.
taken with a dream
a sighting
of her lovely lover
      who is coming down,
           running, down
to meet her where she's waiting
in her pond, in her lake, in her sea.
we could see her waiting
     for the time to be
        her time.
her arms ready to rise
her knees beginning to open, to lift,
we said: she's waking to love.
after so long a time
the sleeping one awakens.
what will that mean?
looking into each other's eyes,
the question spun between us,
glimmered in the softlight,
thoughts, butterflies, moths, soft wings dipping
between our lips, our eyes:

        know this:
   the woman of the earth.
   the woman of the sky.
   the woman of the water,
   of the seaspray.
   the fog.
   wakes.

will pour down
               in the mountain soil.
will descend
               on the limbs of fallen trees.
will blow free
               in the sleet,
                      the blizzard winds
wrapped in white as becomes one just awakened.

     the woman of the hives, of the bees;
     the woman of the cocoon, the butterflies;
     the woman of the coiling meanders, the time
     the woman of the snaking fires, the flame
     the woman of the water, the snow, the rain.

the woman whose waking means
wonder.
water.
want and need.
and her awakening is not death or war, not rage.
she's in love, that woman the world. she's in love.

NAOMI REPLANSKY
The Oasis

I thought I held a fruit cupped in my hand.
Its sweetness burst
And loosed its juice. After long traveling,
After so long a thirst,
     I asked myself: Is this a drought-born dream?
     It was no dream.

I thought I slipped into a hidden room
Out of harsh light.
In cushioned dark, among rich furnishings,

There I restored my sight.
> Such luxury could never be for me!
> It was for me.

I thought I touched a mind that fitted mine
As bodies fit,
Angle to curve; and my mind throbbed to feel
The pulsing of that wit.
> This comes too late, I said. It can't be true!
> But it was true.

I thought the desert ended, and I felt
The fountains leap.
Then gratitude could answer gratitude
Till sleep entwined with sleep.
> Despair once cried: No passion's left inside!
> It lied. It lied.

SUSAN SHERMAN

A Poem

> for you alone
built word upon word
> like years
like time people share
> > together
> deepening
growing into meaning
> > word
> upon word
> > meaning
> upon meaning
for you alone a poem

I know your need for form
for things to be

concrete
the way grass moves & light
the borders
of your shoes
the mountains
of your home
all these things
a kind of boundary
a definition
a name

if I could offer you the salt taste
of the sea
if I could turn your home
into a glance
a gesture
of the eyes
if I could look at you as home
speak to you as sea

there is nothing on this earth
that does not change
that does not deepen or drift
away

there is nothing on this earth
more concrete
than this feeling
I have
now
for you

nothing
is more
real

MURIEL RUKEYSER
The Transgress

That summer midnight under her aurora
northern and still we passed the barrier.

Two make a curse, one giving, one accepting.
It takes two to break a curse

transformed at last in each other's eyes.

I sat on the naked bed of space,
all things becoming other than what they seem

in the night-waking, in the revelation
thundering on tabu after the broken

imperative, while the grotesque ancestors fade
with you breathing beside me through our dream:

bed of forbidden things finally known—
art from the symbol struck, living and made.

Branch lifted green from the dead shock of stone.

THE

ORDER

OF

LOVE

"Meeting" (Margaret Randall)

DIRECTIONS
UNCHOSEN AND CHOSEN

When women enter into a relationship there are usually two basic expectations: the pleasure of a shared intimacy and companionship; the desire for regular satisfying sex. (Some partners make a mutual decision to be celibate and have a companionate relationship. This works when it is truly mutual.)

Once a couple begins to settle into a routine together, old business from childhood may emerge and take over. As the light of love recedes, feelings of unity and closeness may recede. The unchosen path usually goes unrecognized. Jacqueline Lapidus laments:

> *we ignore*
> *the rain, the leaking roof*
>
> *like paint our promises begin*
> *to blister   the ceiling cracks*
> *suspicion seeps through the wall*

The unchosen direction may lead one or both partners to play out patterns that cause evermore conflict or ennui. Chrystos protests battering in

> *What Did He Hit You With? The Doctor Said*
>
> *Shame   Silence*
> *Not he*
> *She*

Melanie Kaye/Kantrowitz describes a standoff:

> *we could talk*
> *but only one of us*
> *will*

Familiar dynamics become entrenched. The relationship plunges into disorder. Judy Grahn validates the emptiness inside the illusion of satisfaction:

> *O What shall I do now that I have*
> *what I've always been looking for.*

Lust or fights may keep things going. But it is a cold, discomforted existence. This is not the way it was supposed to be.

This is not the way it has to be. The second half of this section, directions chosen, illustrates the paths toward love triumphant. May Swenson's "Good Things Come From Thee" is an appreciation:

> *You're strong, you twist off the lids of jars.*
> *Cold nights you're a stove in bed.*

Gale Jackson tenderly details a day in the life of a lesbian mother:

> *she got red lace curtains*
> *love sleep over regular*
> *something from the welfare*
> *a good head on her shoulders*
> *and her little boy*

All sensual pleasures are heightened as love deepens. The wondrous aesthetics of nature are brought into focus by Janice Gould as she takes her lover's hand:

> *Overhead, blackbirds flock*
> *and flock, coming together*
>
> *like the sides of a squeeze-box,*
> *scattering apart, a rush*
>
> *of stars navigating*
> *their own universe.*

Kim Vaeth enjoys picturing her lover in her hot bath on a cold night:

> *your red hair, your red hair*
> *sings to me*

> *through the closed door and the steam*
> *which seeps out*
> *under it.*

A guest house on Cape Cod. Two women alone. Time suspended. A crescendo of passion swells. Alvia Golden Becka sings to her goodly partner:

> *"I love you" under her breath and moves*
> *over and under my body as easily as if we were dancers*
> *and I look down—*
> *we glisten, we're gorgeous.*

There are also chosen feelings but unchosen circumstances. Mary Bennett, serving time in prison, gladly meets her girlfriend in the visitor's room.

> *Blue shirt with embroidered flowers on the front. She ironed her jeans for me. She stands up, her short, stocky body shaking a little bit. She is beautiful. Her name is Janet.*

Margaret Randall's situation changes when she wins her citizenship case, which, before being resolved, had kept her love in the closet:

> *I will claim among other rights*
> *your name on my tongue.*
>
> This is my life partner *I introduce you*
> *in the restaurant parking lot. . . .*

When loving feelings are stronger than all the reasons for anger, love has a better chance to stay on course. Although some lovers find themselves embattled all the time, harmony depends on the arts and crafts of communication.

SAPPHO

Thank you, my dear

You came, and you did
well to come: I needed
you. You have made

love blaze up in
my breast—bless you!
Bless you as often

as the hours have
been endless to me
while you were gone

PAT PARKER

A Small Contradiction

It is politically incorrect
        to demand monogamous
            relationships—

It's emotionally insecure
        to seek
            ownership of
            another's soul—
            or body   &
damaging to one's psyche
to restrict the giving and
            taking of love.

    Me, i am
totally opposed to
monogamous relationships
            unless
                i'm
                in love.

BARBARA RUTH
The Politics of Relationships

I want you to be free.
Whether you want to be or not.
I insist on your independence.
Even though it makes you miserable.
I order you.
To think for yourself.

JOAN LARKIN
Stop

I hate it when you
fill my glass up
without asking me.

I always liked
a little
on a plate
in a cup

an egg
with space around it
an orange
with a knife
next to it

a cup
with space above
the coffee

discrete colors
orange   pewter   black

the porcelain glaze on the china
the blue napkin.

I want to keep things
separate. I hate it
when you break my egg.
I hate when you salt things
when you assume
I want cream

or the shade down
or touch, or looks
of kindness.

I want nothing
to lose
its cutting edge
nothing
to run together.

You had better
stop
pouring yourself
into my glass.

MELANIE KAYE/KANTROWITZ

When You Won't Fight Back

you flinch
at the ocean of words breaking
against your face

i want to knock you off the bed
for looking so innocent
so pained

you wait
you want me to forget how this started
to lay my face into your neck

this
is a creature in the room with us
squatting between us on the bed

this
is a ball we toss back & forth
back & forth,   i

am my mother, scolding
i say, *it won't go away*
you say, *I know*, like a sullen child

what now?
we could wrestle
but we're afraid

we could talk
but only one of us
will

MI OK SONG BRUINING

Object Relations

FOR R.

Adin:

You touched me
in places I was trying to heal.

You placed your self
in the glimmering darkness—
my memories
of repetition compulsion.

The broken world transformed.

I found comfort
in hearing the low
rhythmic sounds
of your heartbeat

listening to the echoes
of your own despair
reflecting my own sorrow.

I walked, I drove, I slept, I drank
and tasted you, searching

for places,
for a safe holding environment—
for signs not spoken,
but in the silence

silent, toxic secrets of your own
hunger and desperation
for better and for more.

I sought refuge
in the haunted place
behind your ghost eyes,
to feel the fragility
of your guarded tenderness

the unhealed scars
from your Ukrainian past
mirroring my own Korean past

losses and empathic failures
revealed a defended truth
we frantically attempted
to escape
into magical thinking,
into each other.

I dreamt of suicide and birth

of being lost, waiting
to be found and taken
to the solace
of your breast.

I betrayed myself
with the wish fulfillment
of our collective lies—
our own primal wounds
and years of hollow
deprivations.

Your latent desires
and shame-based passion
were the only deceptions
you willingly offered.

Dva:

I am convinced
that I am just an object
to relate to
when you have a few moments
to spare, to soothe
the chronic aching,
the lingering emptiness
in your disemboweled life.

I have been mistaken
by these moments
as expressions
of your longing and lust.

I run, I hold my breath,
I sing and dance for you,
I learn a few words
of the language

you were born with—*Pah-roo-ski,*

but I will never
enter you.

There is no time, no way,
no now, no future.
There is no nothing
anymore.

So, please do not.
I cannot, anymore.

(In Ukrainian)
Adin One
Dva Two
Pah-roo-ski Russian

CHRYSTOS
What Did He Hit You With? *The Doctor Said*

Shame   Silence
Not he
She
I didn't correct him
Curled into myself like a bound foot
I looked at the floor ceiling evading
A fist
Hand that has spread me open Fingers I've taken inside me
Screaming   *I love you bitch*   You are the she who rocked
my head side to side
barrier reef for your rage boat
It's safe to beat me
I've lain under your tongue between your thighs
hungry
When I grabbed you to throw you off
you shouted   *If you've scarred my face bitch*
I'll kill you!

I'm sorry   I wept *I didn't mean to scratch you*
Should have said you won't have a chance to kill me
I'm gonna kill you for thinking you can hit me like that
screaming that you love me
You said   *I haven't hit a woman in 8 years*
8 years bad luck my head caught it
My arms in dishwater scrubbing out my father's shoe
The dream tells me you're familiar
brutality I slide into without a horn
You don't have to be beaten to be loved   the therapist said
I held the cool shock of those words
against the purple bruise of still wanting you
You've hit me with that irresistible
deadly weapon
hatred dressed in the shoes & socks of the words
I love you

BECKY BIRTHA

One Room at a Time

I
Kitchen

The kitchen is neutral territory.
Sometimes we can both be here together
          with the lamp in the window lighted
          with supper in the oven
some nights
          this space is close and full
          the whole room warm and alive
and home.

First place in this house
          to feel like our own—
the walls are pine
door and window frames painted orange
cast iron frying pans hang in a line
          by size

down the beam
then the grater, colander, a spare
basket, bunch of
papery dried mint.
The teakettle shrills.

I would call it a truce
the way we spend hours here together
        some nights
drinking coffee
        chocolate, tea.

But there are are no battles
        in this war
we don't fight

only talk

then silence
for long lapses of time.

II
Study

We withdraw to our separate rooms
at the top of the house

I stare for hours
out the window of mine—
        east—
at the facing side of another house:
        a wall of bricks,
at the peak of a church
        against the sky
tumbledown chimneys
the tops of
        renegade ragged ailanthus trees
        sprouted from back gardens
        zig-zag down the block
the broken fence of

our own back garden
littered and strewn
unprotected
in the reckless wind.

III
Living Room

Books, we said
make a room feel
    lived in.
But no one lives in this room.
The couch and chair face
    the ironwork doors of the firebox
    where there is never a fire.
We pass through
    quickly
    on our way between
    the kitchen
and other far parts of the house.

IV
Family Room

We moved the sofa-bed up there and
    the rocking chair
put the sewing machine on a table
    under the window
    by the plants.

It'll be nice for guests, we said
    but we have none.

Cold drafts flow through this room
    whirl up the stairs and
    out at the top
slide in past the single layer of glass
    at the window
push down the chimney and
    through the holes in the fireplace screen.

The plants grow pale and spindly, then
    withered and dry.

V
Bedroom

While we worked it was good.
We moved as a team
    tape, spackle and sand—
you painted, pounded nails,
I mitered corners with the coping saw.
Together we put up molding
    all around the top of the walls:
    mellow, dark-stained wood.

Thick brown carpet
and a curtain letting light
    through the door
the orchid posters—
now
this room is secure
square and safe
a cozy enclosure

and the bed
is a wide
no one's land
where we never kiss
each other deep and
long anymore
where
we are afraid and
no longer
make any
love
only
fall asleep
in one another's arms.

AUDRE LORDE
Walking Our Boundaries

This first bright day has broken
the back of winter.
We rise from war
to walk across the earth
around our house
both stunned that sun can shine so brightly
after all our pain
Cautiously we inspect our joint holding.
A part of last year's garden still stands
bracken
one tough missed okra pod clings to the vine
a parody of fruit cold-hard and swollen
underfoot
one rotting shingle
is becoming loam.

I take your hand beside the compost heap
glad to be alive and still
with you
we talk of ordinary articles
with relief
while we peer upward
each half-afraid
there will be no tight buds started
on our ancient apple tree
so badly damaged by last winter's storm
knowing
it does not pay to cherish symbols
when the substance
lies so close at hand
waiting to be held
your hand
falls off the apple bark
like casual fire
along my back
my shoulders are dead leaves

waiting to be burned
to life.

The sun is watery warm
our voices
seem too loud for this small yard
too tentative for women
so in love
the siding has come loose in spots
our footsteps hold this place
together
as our place
our joint decisions make the possible
whole.
I do not know when
we shall laugh again
but next week
we will spade up another plot
for this spring's seeding.

ALMITRA DAVID

Medusa

when first I heard the
hissing in my hair
I called it a laugh
and left it at that—
there was breakfast to be made

now the earth
lies hot
in the afternoon sun
I feel it against my back
lying here   face to the sky
I see
what is sprouting from my head

my fingers slide through
my hair   back to the
pond where I sat
pleased as the lilies   and knowing
back to that day when
my blood and
the stream and
the pond flowed together
I stood no smaller than
the mountain   my hair
moving with the clouds

in the dark you
stroke me and say how
smooth I am   how
there is nothing rough to
offend your hands

when this morning's sun
warmed the bed   my hair
moved on the pillow   you
saw me   the light
shining through my hair   you
came toward me and
stopped   stood
in front of me as
still as stone

CHERYL CLARKE
Untitled

i.
How much I do want you
all the time   for my
self   never out of my
legs   nights pushing

between your thighs is
relentless, infinite waking,
primordial   nights without
you   dark is sorrowful   mornings
forgetful of dreams.

ii.
For me I want my body's
freedom to protect the narrowness
and breadth and danger of
my own bed.

CHERRÍE MORAGA

Where Beauty Resides

*Maya mathematics from the beginning of the Classic Period included . . .
the concept of zero, principally as a symbol of completeness.*
MIGUEL LEÓN PORTILLA

1
Your hand, a cup
that empties me
of myself.
I am reduced
to zero.
I meditate on how I will live
without reflection.

The quiet invades.

Thursday morning and minutes ago you were here with me.
I look out onto a city of grey and steel blue structures
I spot you folded into one of them
red brick lining the walls where you work
you are thinking of me
you put pencil to your lip
teeth imbedded into knuckle

you inhale
what was once me or the scent of your own
expectant
desire.

Here, indoors, the city is not grey
the sheets are a steel blue that ignite your eyes
searching me strip searching me,
I have gone no more
your hand has only emptied me of all want.
"Satisfecha," I say the word hard like sex
whole in meaning.

When you rise I watch you
cover your body
your elbows spread like crooked wings
bra snaps behind your back
you step into panties
sliding up thighs
your wound mouth disappears
shirt slipping over head
you emerge, a radiant medusa.

I see you as I was instructed to,
"you have a beautiful body"
you smile, snap up the crotch
of your jeans . . .
but your beauty resides elsewhere
you know this too
emptied of ourselves.

9

I only ask this one thing of you:
Beyond woman hidden in woman
resides child hidden in child
resides zero.

There is no loneliness there
but a strangeness, I admit

my eyes scanning the cityscape for your shape
against the fog's haze, I search
strip search these words
emptied of myself.

2
*"A cup is molded of clay
but its . . . hollow space
is the useful part."**

As a catholic schoolgirl I would have confessed
the sin of you   my body, a temple
the temple of my undoing.

I suspect this feeling is called sadness
I suspect I used to name this loneliness
your back walking out the door
the weight of another being as fragile
as delicate as lonely as mine
heavy upon your shoulders.

I think of others, too, while I kiss you,
pacts we make in the stolen hours of urban life.
I'll promise you anything
for the bowl of your breasts and thighs
to contain me once more this morning this bed.

I am speaking of something else here
with no name
it is about the number zero
without loneliness betrayal regret
you emptied me of myself.

O

When you leave, what I remember as fear
a vague sense of relief
a panicked moment of abandonment

*Carolyn Merchant, *Radical Ecology: The Search for a Livable World.*

what I remember in myriad
faces of lovers at myriad
numbers of doors in myriad
faceless numberless cities
dissipates from me
I watch you leave emptied of those memories
I watch you leave and enter me
my eyes, liquid
prey before her hunter.

Return to me, amor, again
and again with the same animal hunger.
I will not refuse you I have nothing left to lose.
You cannot devour what is infinite you drink
until replenished and drink again
and I am the receiver of your thirst
your tongue, my blessing
your hands, gifts from the gods.

I am emptied of myself.
Relieved of this burden.
My body a sacrament,
a flame
a holy sacrifice.

All else is blasphemy.

3
I am writing you to reach you without words
you will not read these words as much as you will see them
this day written in the bay grey sky
you will know me better than you imagined
forgive me everything
and the generosity will lay upon us
span the bridge that links and divides us

and I could go on writing like this forever
only guessing
at what lies inside
the shape and size of these letters.

JACQUELINE LAPIDUS
Living Together

we agree we do not own
each other   there is space
for her where I live

I clear old lovers off the shelves
carefully she unpacks her habits,
spoons confidence into cups

I open myself like a window
she breathes deeply
we get high on each other's skin

houseproud, we forget the building's
old and shaky   we ignore
the rain, the leaking roof

like paint our promises begin
to blister   the ceiling cracks
suspicion seeps through the wall

can we cover it with plaster? how
can we be sure it will not
fall on us while we sleep?

ROBIN BECKER
In Conversation

When your name comes up
in conversation over dinner,
I come to your defense.
She looked beautiful, someone said,
but unsettled. She left a suitcase

in the shed. As if you left me here
to cover—an extra ear, hand, eye—
or to mount your reputation.
I know what I know from experience:
you were a strong swimmer;
you defected from your family;
you made love like a person
who had to catch a plane.
By the end of the meal, you're larger
than life, an outlaw with class.
When we gather before the fire,
couples lie in each other's arms,
those alone climb into themselves.
Like a diligent agent
stationed in a foreign country,
I'm waiting for a signal
to come home.

JUDY GRAHN

Love came along   and saved me saved me

Love came along   and saved me saved me
Love came along and
after that I did not feel like fighting for
anything anymore after all
didnt I have   not that I had
anything to speak of
OR keep quiet about
but didnt I have
company in my nothing?
someone to say You're Great, to shout you are
wonderful, to whisper to me you are my every little thing?
& then one day Love left to go save someone else.
Love ran off with all my self-esteem my sense of being
wonderful and all my nothing.
now I am in the hole.

JUDY GRAHN
Love came along and saved me

Love came along and saved me
saved me   saved
me.
However, my life remains the same as before.
O What shall I do now that I have
what I've always been looking for.

MARGARET RANDALL
Breaking Out
FOR BARBARA

I
There were always those who had eyes to see
who understood the real meaning of the word *housemate*
deciphered the codes our words and hands
spoke across distance, a street, a room, a telephone wire.

We never said *lover* or *partner*
except by mistake
or within a silent circle
louder and spreading
as more trusted friends entered the safety of its space.

At first it was top secret
hugged to frightened breastbones
we vowed we would do this and more
for years, a lifetime if necessary.

They wanted me out because of what I speak, write,
because I won't say *I'm sorry*
or promise never to do it again.
And this love of ours is also branded deportable.

They wanted me out and I fought, we fought
telling no one
as the circle enveloped a nation
our galaxy burning out of sight.

II
Now that I've won this case am judged a citizen
—was always one, they say—
I will claim among other rights
your name on my tongue.

This is my life partner I introduce you
in the restaurant parking lot. *I miss you*
I tell you on the phone
remembering that was one of the phrases
we sometimes allowed ourselves
when we turned the needles of pain to rage and hoped
that blind to our womanlove
they'd think we were just two friends
missing each other
missing each other so much.

Having come home we are free
to say our passion loud
here on reclaimed land
identify ourselves
share in the blasphemed freedom
enjoyed by every lesbian and gay man in the USA.

MARILYN HACKER
Runaways Café II

For once, I hardly noticed what I ate
(salmon and broccoli and Saint-Véran).
My elbow twitched like jumping beans; sweat ran
into my shirtsleeves. Could I concentrate

on anything but your leg against mine
under the table? It was difficult,
but I impersonated an adult
looking at you, and knocking back the wine.
Now that we both want to know what we want,
now that we both want to know what we know,
it still behooves us to know what to do:
be circumspect, be generous, be brave,
be honest, be together, and behave.
At least I didn't get white sauce down my front.

JANICE GOULD
Blackbirds

At dusk we start home
through the wet fields.

Overhead, blackbirds flock
and flock, coming together

like the sides of a squeeze-box,
scattering apart, a rush

of stars navigating
their own universe.

The birds whisper in the damp air,
their wings breathe.

When you take my hand
I feel the pulse of their flight

in my throat, my chest.
I feel their pull

flutter through you.

MARY BENNETT
My Girlfriend

See, my girlfriend comes to see me sometimes. When they let her in. When they figure I deserve it. She's waiting for me in the visiting room. The guard brings me. She's sitting there so pretty, her black hair tied behind her neck, bushy and wavy across her back, tied with fat red yarn. She's got the sweetest face, smiling at me, that tooth still missing in the front. She holds her hand up to her face, like she wants to hide that missing tooth. She lost it in a fight. Her old man beating her up. She wouldn't take that no more, hit him back, bloodied his nose. She ran away. I found her in a bar. That sweet face, smiling. I took her home. When I close my eyes, I remember the smell of her that first night. She cried. Told me she never been with a woman, why didn't she know it was so good? My girlfriend, when I see her, makes me remember every little thing we did together. Every word we talked. She's waiting for me in the visiting room. Blue shirt with embroidered flowers on the front. She ironed her jeans for me. She stands up, her short, stocky body shaking a little bit. She is beautiful. Her name is Janet. Janet is my girlfriend. I love her. No one else comes to see me here. I try to look my best for Janet. Make sure my hair is combed and braided smooth. I can't wear the cologne I used to wear outside. But Janet doesn't care. We hold hands and sometimes we cry. Her eyes are brown and so deep, I could take a journey in them. And oftentimes I did. She promises to get me out of here, but I know that's impossible. So, my girlfriend comes to see me here. It's too bad. We should be free. Running down the sidewalk. Shouting and laughing. Maybe one day. If they ever want to. But every week, I get to see Janet for one hour. It's good to see her.

JO WHITEHORSE COCHRAN
Morning Étude
FOR JUDY

A blue heron lifts
from the hill-enclosed bay.
A fog laps back
on the rock
the heron left.

Near the window,
she turns to the coming morning.
The line of her body
follows that rising ease,
the blue arc of wing
darker than water.

She flattens a palm
to the lead-glass pane,
as if a touch
would hold the heron.

KIM VAETH
The Bath

Only the sound of you
        splashing while I shift
                from foot to foot in the cold
kitchen where the windows
        have frosted so I can't see out.
                I pull the strong overhead and light
floods the cold, hard surfaces
        each time, too bright.
                You are taking one of your famous

baths, as you do

        when you are tired or cold

                or uneasy in the night. Newly washed,

your red hair, your red hair

        sings to me

                through the closed door and the steam

which seeps out

        under it.

                I know it is late but your hair

is not tired. And though I am very

        cold, I am happy

            being sung to.

Soon, but not yet,

        I will walk into the bathroom,

            sit down on the blue toilet seat

and ask you something.

        You in the tub,

            naked and wet, your skin

shining and freckled,

        your eyes closed, your glasses far away

            in another room, your singing hair

swept back by water,

        converging where your nape

            curves into the tub's curve, a thin washcloth

spread over your chest.

JEWELLE GOMEZ
For Mi Osita

In sleep she arches a brow
over her dark shadowed eye,
causing ripples
that move out from her center
to encircle me.
Light sneaks into our shuttered room.
The scented air lingers on the copper of her skin
and the coal black of her curls.
Her sleeping hums in my ear
closing out noise of the traffic below
and Monday to come,
harmonizing with the rustle of the sheet
as she turns her back to me.
An invitation I always recognize.

GALE JACKSON
conversations with love
another one.

she got red lace curtains
love sleep over regular
something from the welfare
a good head on her shoulders
and her little boy
in the apartment on third avenue
what's left of industrial brooklyn
where a harbor calls traffic beeps
and immigrant dreams go
to impatience in a window box
and write on the walls who will not
be nameless
she got red lace curtains against

the grays and blues
she wears a chain of gold
and a chain of half possible dreams
among the people on the buses
dreams curvaceous as sea shells
or the lover's sleeping form
or the gold chain in her blouse
among the people on the streets
in the buses
unseen
but known knowing waiting bursting
to bloom
she comes home from the sewing kicks
off her shoes
and this poem is hers on her feet
the bus the exhaust where the two highways
cross over her clothesline two women's intimates
little boy briefs and the arrogant smell
of cuchifritos and factories for miles
and miles
and this poem is hers like the curtains
to flaunt like love at night pumps
for dancing gold hidden sneakers for work
back and forth back and forth morenita
a cup of coffee a prayer a wing.

HONOR MOORE
Shenandoah

Photograph: Breakfast after our first full night:
Elbow on the table, fist against your face, intent
    on the cup you look into. Your hair glints
        in three-year-old light.
In these rooms of borrowed furniture, white
walls, wide windows that curve, I have been solitary.
    A cymbidium orchid. Artichokes. Fresh
        trout. I tear pink netting from
the orchid, float it. Red wine is breathing. A plane
lands hours away, and I can think of you driving
    a valley roofed with clouds, your voice
        like the charge of new weather.

Yesterday, eyes shut, sun on my face, I could
remember you viscerally: Heat, sun that caressed
    our naked skin, blond grasses, weeds baked
        to vivid rust. There was no
snow—odd that far north in late October. From ours
other mountains were feathery with bare trees
    and some phenomenon of light turned
        their billowing crests
lavender. See those mountains make a giant sprawled
on her back: those, breasts; the one called Otter, torso.
    See the lake bright near her cheek, the
        trout stream etch her chin.

I am afraid in the vestibule, your face
smiling its guileless welcome. I want to cry, hold you,
    open through your breasts into safe billowing
        darkness. I kiss you
as if we are just friends. I lead you through
white rooms. I hand you the orchid because I cannot
    tell you. You reach. I start, as if your touch were
        too much light. I trim
the artichokes. The red wine breathes. I must cover

the curved windows. In this valley roofed with clouds, I live
alone in rooms on a street where
all the shades are pulled.

We drink red wine. We unbutton, touch. We eat
trout—clouded eye, clear black night shut from the house, petal
flush of your skin. We eat artichokes, mark
leaf after leaf with our teeth.
The orchid floats. It is your darkness I want with my
mouth. If I could speak as sound not edged into
word, I could tell you. Leaves now: two, four,
five at once. We reach
center, loose lavender-streaked swirl, split the naked
heart in the night bed where I speak with my hands
and we breathe, mouth to mouth, unedged,
shorn to simple tenderness.

NAOMI REPLANSKY

Fragment of a Night

That curved carved mouth,
That tender much-inventing wandering mouth!
I could say more. But now my lips are sealed.

JUDITH MCDANIEL

From Body of Love
Buck Mountain, Lake George

III.
We climbed that mountain in the snow,
the three of us. Do you remember?
How our boots were soaked through
after the first half-mile, but we
slogged on, holding ourselves carefully
in the iced spots, thinking to show
your son the view from the windblown summit
of his first mountain.

We stopped at a waterfall, splashed with ice lace,
delicate as a snowflake, not quite concealing
deep and cold rushing water. I line you up
for a picture, your son by your side, the grey
rock rising behind you. A winter perfect picture,
all tones of grey and white and dark mossy greens
in the water and pine trees, your son by your side,
his lean young body repeating yours. I paused
and looked around the camera to check this image,
then pressed the shutter. But the camera
took no picture.

We fussed with it briefly, then threw it
in the pack, shrugged, and went on climbing.
At the top we found only mist and dark clouds,
no amazing view to entice this boy to climb again.
Yet we had a wonderful day, do you remember?
He will not soon forget the climb, the summit
with no view, and I will remember a photograph
that exists only in me: that moment when I
looked around the camera and saw you,
saw winter close around your frosted skin,
saw dark water rushing through you,
saw your hand resting easily on your son's shoulder.

MAY SWENSON

Good Things Come From Thee

On the Cliff

I'm sawing a slice off that hard dark knobby loaf
from Zabar's—black molasses and raisins in it—
to have with Tilsit cheese. You left a pumpkin and
autumn leaves on the stripped wood table, you filled
the birdfeeder hanging from the eaves. The window
is clean, the sill is varnished, white impatiens
in a brick clay pot smile above the sink. Our terrace
lined with boulders, the slate path with pachysandra
you planted. Storm doors are on, in front and back
it's snug in here. I'm chewing, looking at the shelves
you cut and hung to hold our books and decoys.
You're strong, you twist off the lids of jars.
Cold nights you're a stove in bed.

By the Canal

For Valentine's Day a whole studio and library!
Shelves built to the ceiling, there's space for every
thing: papers, folders, files and books, books, books.
Binoculars and chess set, tape recorders, tapes and
jigsaw. Telephone that's a blue car has a shelf
of its own. The old maple sawhorse table fits right in
and looks brand new. Curly ivy on the sill and outside
an entire alphabet of birds, on the porch, in the yard.
You put pink ribbons of sunrise in the back window,
scarlet bands of sunset in the front, the moon above our
bed at night. It snowed. You made a path. The Christmas
poinsettia blooms all year.

GEORGIA HEARD
Play It Slower

Your eyes like a lake on a windy day. They wouldn't stay still. Your
mouth like the mountains behind. I wanted to kiss that day, so soft.
Your breath came louder and louder. We sailed. You held me. Watched
my brown shoulder. We both were afraid. I kept pushing inside you. It
began to rain. The storm came slowly from behind the mountains.
You trembled beneath me. I fucked you slowly. We held onto each
other. What else is there? The birds scatter themselves together one
body sensing which shape to make, which edge to pull in, to make it
whole, even the wind is whole. Who is going to pull in the net? With
the fish so slippery moving inside?

> Her fluffy citadel. Her nest.
> Her orange bird feather. Lifted up
> wings. A curtain. A flavor.
> A side dish perhaps. A lock and
> key. A knob. No, a beak.
> Drums. An angle I never expected.
> A dish. A month. A compass.
> Maps in a book. Panama.

The tree shakes water down. It is not yet drying. The wind laps the
waves. I lap her up. Mountains and the sea. A canary sings. Stars are
like medallions. They wink. Open buds in spring. A bird flies into a
nest. A river inside. A map of the world. Oceans. Continents. The
earth rotates. The ground swells. The bird flies out. A flock of them.
How do they know where they're going? They pull the edges together.
Overseas even. Her mouth open. She shudders and I slow down. Play
it slower.

MELANIE HOPE
Lesbian Bed Day

Some would understand how I can
stay here in bed with you
on a day when the sun
is bursting wide open and wet
in the sky—hollering
down to the people,
". . . it's your thang
do what you wanna do
I can't tell you
who to sock it to . . ."

And here we are
with a mug of water
and the belief that outside
will still be outside
when we are through
loving, sucking, and squushing
each other—
and if not, it may well be
worth the sacrifice for this
shapeless orgasmic
moment in time.

Those who don't understand
have not hugged
the rugged bark of trees
and heard them answer—
they have not heard you
when you sleepily say:
"I'll be here
when you get back."

After a while
it doesn't matter
who understands,

because not everyone wants
to open themselves
at the bottom
and let someone look inside.

ALVIA G. GOLDEN
Acts of Love

Sweat can be magical.
When I'm sun-tanned the deep reddish brown
of my Hungarian mother, so my arms look strong,
passionate, wrapped around Becka's fair Irish body,
and I'm telling her the kind of story she likes,
with nuns and little girls in lace panties,
or one with a big woman in a stiff uniform,
any of the ones that make her start to move her ass
rhythmically and lock her legs around me and improve
the plot unexpectedly—then when we work up a sweat
it feels so good it's supernatural.
Like now, in this sweet little guest house
on a drought-yellow Cape Cod afternoon
with a hint of breeze blowing across us
from one window to the other, when Becka cries
"Yes!" and "God, yes!" quietly, hoarsely into my ear
and thrusts herself against me and sings
"I love you" under her breath and moves
over and under my body as easily as if we were dancers
and I look down—
we glisten, we're gorgeous.

BARBARA DEMING

From Norma/1933–1934

1.
she held the flower cold up against her cheek
bones in the dark the petals flattened cold up
against her cheekbones this flower your
fingers you had danced with this flower in your
mouth your tongue had been pink like a cat's
tongue and slender touching the petals you had
danced with this flower in your mouth held in
your teeth your teeth biting the petals the
petals cold up against her cheekbones she held
the flower cold up against her cheekbones in
the dark.

4.
wet earth to my lips
i sing
o and to touch her breasts with gentle fingers
o and to touch
      slant-fingered
      o
      and to touch slant-thrill-fingered
      her warm breasts

i weep to o wet earth and my fingers
where my fingers sing
ohgodohgodohgodohgodohgodohgod

SUZANNE GARDINIER
Where Blind Sorrow Is Taught To See
Book Three

It's Independence Day or by now
Independence Night I have waited for you
so long The day's heat rises from the streets
but the breeze will come if we pull the curtains
aside Show me everything We will have
our own speeches and our own processions
our own declarations our own pageants
of union But there will be no banners
and no militia Heard around the world
will be only this Each part of your body
is speaking a different language scapula
clavicle rib nipples soft then hard
against my lips In each language are hundreds
of dialects slangs speech rhythms and
impediments within each of these millions
of tones of human voice and inflection
My only hope of being able
to understand even the smallest part
of the conversation is to draw as close
as I can I turn you on your side
and run my tongue from the small of your back
down slowly over every province
between there and your navel on the other side
and back again and again and again
I listen I circumnavigate the world.

THE

VEXATION

OF

LOVE

"In counsel" (Margaret Randall)

DANGER

HATE

HEALING

L ike all women in contemporary society, lesbians live in a dangerous world. Added to the daily insults and acts of unexpected violence rooted in misogyny and racism, is the widespread fear and loathing for same-sex love.

Danger can occur on the streets, as Minnie Bruce Pratt illustrates:

> *Around the corner screamed*
> *a car, the men, shouts:* Dykes, Dykes. *Have you*
> *ever tried to frighten someone out of their life?*

Danger can occur in the mountains. Rebecca Wight and Claudia Brenner, a young lesbian couple, were shot by a man who stalked them to their tent on the Appalachian Trail.* Rebecca died from a bullet wound that hit her in the back and exploded her liver. This event is engraved by Adrienne Rich in poem V of *An Atlas of the Difficult World:*

> *killing one woman, the other*
> *dragging herself into town   his defense they had teased his*
> *   loathing*
> *of what they were*

Danger also filters into the privacy of our own homes. Joan Larkin traces an attraction to rough sex back to the childhood "Beatings" by mother and father.

> *Her knuckles landed*
> *hard on my shoulders, in my ribs and guts.*
> . . . .

*See Claudia Brenner, *Eight Bullets*, Firebrand Books, 1995.

137

Belt,
brush, or his large hand came down
open and steady

Relationships are threatened by the way we act out hate and recycle childhood memories, from emotional neglect to treachery. Elizabeth Lorde-Rollins explores this dynamic:

> *For my survivor lover*
> *pain has no boundaries*
> *spills to our howling bed*
> . . . .
> *Another memory today.*
> *That uncle offering you to the boy scouts*

As we work our way out of these agonies, love is a road to the restoration of body and soul.

Love and loss are intertwined. Sadness so often bites after the heels of joy. Poems of familiar suffering are frequently experienced as a source of comfort, such as Robin Morgan's sonnet, "Dreaming the Volcano."

> *Then, safe in your smoldering arms, I slept,*
> *at peace. And woke in bed, alone. And wept.*

If we were lucky enough to have been wanted and brought up with good enough nurturing as children, it is easier to feel and express a little routine hate for the person we love. In "Poet to Tiger" May Swenson catalogues the rankles and rattles of her partner with generous humor.

> *You're right. I brought a grain*
> *or two of sand*
> *into bed I guess in my socks.*
> *But it was you pushed them off*
> *along with everything else.*

Occasional fights clear the air and give a relationship breathing space. Jacqueline Lapidus finds her way to "Healing":

> *after each quarrel I*
> *rush into the bedroom*

138

for a good cry
. . . .
I read poems   write poems
healing myself
for overtures   my toes
against her toes

Having affairs, walking out, closing down may seem much easier, but provide only temporary relief and escape. The problems remain. The more secure we are, the less likely we are to be derailed by hate; and the more likely we are to survive the vexations of love. In "Jealousy" Pamela Sneed allows herself

> *a totally unfeministic fantasy*
> *I want to rip her apart*
> *piece*
>
> *by*
>
> *piece*

Must you tell your lover everything? Must you express every fear or fantasy? There is a balance to be found: Withholding every spicy crumb can prevent intimacy; spewing out every crusty nugget can destroy it. The goal is to cultivate a gift for timing, a sense of strategy as one moves between quiet and confrontation.

SAPPHO

After all this

Atthis, you hate
even the thought

of me. You dart
off to Andromeda

ADRIENNE RICH

From "An Atlas of the Difficult World"

V

Catch if you can your country's moment, begin
where any calendar's ripped-off: Appomattox
Wounded Knee, Los Alamos, Selma, the last airlift from Saigon
the ex-Army nurse hitch-hiking from the debriefing center; medal
        of spit on the veteran's shoulder
—catch if you can this unbound land these states without a cause
earth of despoiled graves and grazing these embittered brooks
these pilgrim ants pouring out from the bronze eyes, ears,
           nostrils,
the mouth of Liberty
         over the chained bay waters
                      San Quentin:
once we lost our way and drove in under the searchlights to the
        gates
end of visiting hours, women piling into cars
the bleak glare aching over all
                Where are we moored?   What
                are the bindings?   What be-
                hooves us?

Driving the San Francisco–Oakland Bay Bridge
no monument's in sight but fog
prowling Angel Island muffling Alcatraz
poems in Cantonese inscribed on fog
no icon lifts a lamp here
history's breath blotting the air
over Gold Mountain   a transfer
of patterns like the transfer of African appliqué
to rural Alabama   voices alive in legends, curses
tongue-lashings
            poems on a weary wall

And when light swivels off Angel Island and Alcatraz
when the bays leap into life

              views of the Palace of Fine Arts,

TransAmerica
when sunset bathes the three bridges
                                    still
old ghosts crouch hoarsely whispering
under Gold Mountain

○

North and east of the romantic headlands there are roads into tule
                fog
places where life is cheap poor quick unmonumented
Rukeyser would have guessed it coming West for the opening
of the great red bridge   *There are roads to take* she wrote
when you think of your country   driving south
to West Virginia Gauley Bridge silicon mines the flakes of it
                heaped like snow, death-angel white
—poet journalist pioneer mother
uncovering her country: *there are roads to take*

○

I don't want to know how he tracked them
along the Appalachian Trail, hid close
by their tent, pitched as they thought in seclusion
killing one woman, the other
dragging herself into town   his defense they had teased his
                loathing
of what they were   I don't want to know
but this is not a bad dream of mine   these are the materials
and so are the smell of wild mint and coursing water remembered
and the sweet salt darkred tissue I lay my face
upon, my tongue within.
                        A crosshair against the pupil of an eye
could blow my life from hers
a cell dividing without maps, sliver of ice beneath a wheel
could do the job.   Faithfulness isn't the problem.

MINNIE BRUCE PRATT

#67 To Be Posted on 21st Street, Between Eye and Pennsylvania

FOR JOAN

Take this poem down. You can take it and

read it. I wrote it for you passing by, you
standing at the grey plywood construction
wall where it happened. If you'd been here, what
would you have done? Believe me, it was not fun.

And I had been happy, supper at the Trieste
around the corner, that nice Italian place,
cheap cheese ravioli. Was pleasantly hand
in hand with my lover, walking to Eye and 21st,
back to the car. Happy despite hard glances.
Angled eyes of two women, next table, unused
to seeing two people together like us. But
we went on, happy. It was a triumph of love.
Holding hands in the street's raw pink glow,
a little like the movies, slow motion angle
on us stepping into the flimsy sidewalk tunnel,
tunnel of love, wedding arch, *arc de triomphe*
after the war, secret passage, honeysuckle
arbor, except it was us in the blunt echo
off the boards, laughing, at walk in the city,
Saturday night.
          When some young white men
passed and began to talk at us, derisive.
University, not hard hat, if that's what you
are thinking. Or maybe you're one of them,
reading this now. Why did you try shame?
The mock: *I can't believe it. Can't believe
it. They're holding hands.* Six to us two.
A tongue's scratch scratch, trying to get at
our hearts. Like a movie, sudden threat.
Predictable. I get so tired of this disbelief.

My tongue, faithful in my mouth, said: *Yes, we are.*
The shout: *Lesbians. Lesbians.* Trying to curse
us with our name. Me louder: *That's what we are.*

Around the corner, empty street. Nobody came
with rocks, or dogs. Alone and glad of it,
still holding hands. Around the corner screamed
a car, the men, shouts: *Dykes, dykes.* Have you
ever tried to frighten someone out of their life?
Just having a good time, like shooting at ducks
down by the Bay, or at the office telling jokes.
Nothing personal except to the ones getting hit,
other side of the threat.
                But this is a poem
about love, so I should say: In the torn silence
we stood, in the night street, and kissed, solemn,
sweet as any engagement party or anniversary,
stern as the beginning or end of a country's war,
in the risk of who knows who might come and see
us in the open, isolate, tender, exchanging a kiss,
a triumph like no other.
                I hope you, here,
have read through, didn't crumple or tear this
up the middle at *lesbian.* I hope you carefully
took this poem down and read it. Now it's a poem
about you, about how there can be a triumph of love.

MARY BENNETT
Cells

Cell, brick, cement, bars, walls, hard,
tv's, soaps, stories, tears, no visitors
allowed, lawyers, liars, guards, big,
touch guns, mean fingers, small bed,
green cloth, disinfectant, toilet, sink,
bars, no window, no door, no knob to turn,

no air, no wind, cold, nightmares, screams,
no touch, no touching.

> I want to touch someone. I want to hold
> that woman who cries every goddam night.

I WANT TO TOUCH SOMEONE.

JOAN LARKIN

Beatings

They beat me different ways.
My mother was standing
in her light summer suit and hat.
She was late; it was my fault.
She was almost sobbing. A cord
was twisted around her breath,
an animal trying to escape
from her throat. Her knuckles landed
hard on my shoulders, in my ribs and guts.
Her face was close. She was yelling,
yanking me by the hair, and I saw
my brother she'd sent to bring me home
standing near us in the hall, watching.
Standing and forgetting why he was there
watching and what he liked about it.

I was younger. I think we were all there,
four or five in the kitchen, father home
for supper between shifts. He lifted me
over his knees to hit me. Belt,
brush, or his large hand came down
open and steady on both buttocks, burning
and stinging through thin underpants,
big voice in control, saying This
is for your own good, This
hurts us, This is because we love you.

I cannot remember my crime, only my face
against his knees.   His hands, his strong
voice telling me I was loved.

When the man beat me later
in the bed in Brooklyn, the kind man
with big lips and hands, the man
who loved me and beat me
with the same voice, when years later
in the same bed, the thin woman with tattooed
wrists told me I couldn't receive
love, thrusting the dildo till I was
sore and crying Stop, she laughing,
shouting I couldn't love her—
it wasn't true.   I loved the rising
of their voices—his dark, steady one,
sure, in control, and her demented one
rising like my dead mother's wild voice
telling of love and pain, how both once
stood in the house and were punished together.

CHRYSTOS
Against

your skin red under my hand against every
political principle we both hold you want
me to spank you & I do
We're survivors of childhood violence with black eyes
in common from mothers who hated our difference
Neither loves our love
they'd beat it out of us if they could
Your people as well as mine slaughtered in millions
Queer we're still open season
My fingermarks on your ass are loving you
tied to the bed my other hand pushing
into our vortex of pleasure   I'd agree that it's wrong
to do this

Out of our bruised lives should come some other way
This forbidden hand this deep memory this connection
for which I've no explanation against a wall of right
that would define us as victim/aggressor
I want to give you
what you want
although my kind would beat it out of me with words
if they could
My hands guess this is a difference that is a crime
to admit in our small queer world
Desire red & raw as wounds we disguise
we're open season

LANUOLA ASIASIGA
Untitled

Do you know what it's like
To have to try and make love
With someone you care about
Someone you really love
And in the middle of it all
You hate her
Hate her to death
For reminding you
For triggering the memories
You've buried so deep

ELIZABETH LORDE-ROLLINS
Living Through It

I.
For my survivor lover
pain has no boundaries
spills to our howling bed

my finger and I stiff and furious
finally arriving to an empty cold coming
without her.

I sleep with your five-year-old ghost
know her
by the bitemarks on her arm and the adolescent
rapists on her back
while the grown-up keeps me
waiting / on my knees
come share my dirty secrets
I dream I licked her and she liked it
she asks for more / in my dreams
I search my own house for a place to masturbate
find some dark corner, then get caught.
She sleeps.
Desire hot and wet keeps me
up and always ready to be bad
begging the air for a way out.

if you love me
you won't need

II.
The children are waiting outside
in protecting mother arms
and this girl baby, fever for a week
on the table.
Mami and sister and
brother play with her
toes and belly
the diaper is on, then off
children fascinated at her peeing genitals

I can't help staring at this seven year old brother
he's adorable as he makes cooing noises gently in her face
he'll be fourteen in seven years
fourteen like that babysitter's son
I shoo the children out
"we're going to examine your sister now, please

wait outside"
Mother frowns and the attending doc
looks disapproving.
After the examination the doctor gives reassurance
"she'll be just fine . . . ," and looking at me pointedly
"I can see she's got a very loving family."

The world is full of loving families.
New ones every day.

III.
Another memory today.
That uncle offering you to the boy scouts
an artificial respiration dummy
each boy around the table
returns to your mouth like a minute hand
these are not small deaths
even I can't bring you back
pull myself away drowning in all
the whirlpool bedrooms we've ever
torn down the middle
I am not those boys
wake up do you hear me

if you love me
you won't ask me to do this thing with you

IV.
OK so after five years I needed someone
OK???!!!
I'm not your fucking compañera
I'm your *fucking* compañera
and how the hell did I end up
the bad guy, after five years
my wanting making me   the babysitter's son
another uncle?
I was your lover
and I need I need I need my dirty deeds
When solitary mornings drop like pins
on our bathroom's tiled floor

I am there to meet them: my head against the bathtub
conjuring pricks to keep me company
coming in an endless rainbow
stroking and sucking and some of them mine
buried in some *Torso* boy's succulent ass
I need I need I NEED
our bodies meeting gentle
then urgent
lying at your breast sweaty and exhausted
your taste warm and generous on my lips.
But I can't think about you on these mornings.
I need to come
I cry instead.

I can kill now.
I wish I'd been there I'd exterminate that goddamn living room
where they rode your childish body
til you swore off for good.
Shit I wish I coulda gotten them out of our bedroom
sixteen years and they're tighter on you than an iron girdle
Headless horsemen still taking your sex
from you, from me.

if you love me
you won't want anyone else.

V.
You hate me for sleeping with her
making it
as expensive as possible.
You should thank me
my aches for you no longer whistle through your hallways
carrying dead leaves of kisses we had
and we are alive to see the sun this morning
from different beds
I have survived your rage
you have survived
my need.

Viewings I

Six months later we run into each other at the Queer Film Fest.
You've shaved your head, something you know I can't resist.

When they let us inside I retreat to a far-away aisle.
The lights dim, balcony a black chasm between us.
The dark, though intangible, is an insistent presence.

In the first scene
boys' and girls'
inviting asses
invite black rubber,
lube and rubber gloves.
"Master" flashes on the screen
intersecting sex and text.
Girls go down on each other's cocks,
go down on their knees
licking black Doc Martens clean.
Then sea anemones, swimming pools, steam.

Six months later,
here in porn's soft core,
you're still the star of my show.

Remember the night I wrote on you in lipstick,
how the lipstick left a stain?
The sheets were full of expletives for days.
Handcuffs. Hands clasped in hair.
Tongues like rings down fevered drains.
My desire for you is still crowned in that flame
like the MGM lion clawing out of his frame.

Scene two: back seat caresses, strap-ons, cowgirls and lassos,
pirate suits, anchors, and punk boys with tattoos.
All backdropped by the rhythms that you used to fuck me to.

But when the handsome dyke in the last frame
stroking her girlfriend's cock
urgently murmurs, "Thank you, Daddy,"
I remember why we're sitting
in this dark so far apart,
what's pushed up against us—
intangible, insistent.
Not these sexy games, but him.

BESSY REYNA

On the Battlefield of Your Body

I.
The last time we used
silence
as bullets,
we were mortally wounded
in the conflict.

Now, we have scarcely begun
to recuperate,
and our rifles are already
cocked for battle.

Incapable of admitting
defeat,
we once again confront each other
on the battlefield
of your body.

II.
In the shadows,
hiding between your hands,
I forget to be afraid.
With you I cross the frontier of
desire,

penetrate the territory
where life and death dissolve.

Shipwrecked,
but still thirsty for adventure,
I submerge myself
in the turbulence
of your waters.
Ambushed again.

MAYA ISLAS

From Details of a Violent Saint

11
My inner wave is a moving sea;
a myth evaporating the strength of women.
Soft body dies suddenly
and falls somewhere,
among the cracks of a patriarchal universe.

I carry my arrow and shoot every face I see.
I shoot beards and hairy legs,
insensitive navels joining together
                    I shoot.

I need Buddhism; I need a lama
who speaks to me about the impermanence of things.
All is white.
        All is nothing.
A monk will open my heart and he will take you out.
Your whole body and soul will dwell outside me,
and he will make a butter sculpture out of you
to prove again that we do not exist as we think,
and then,
I'll buy bread
and spread your essence over my breakfast.

PAT PARKER

From Love Poems

Bitch!
i want to scream
I hate you
Fuck you for this pain
You used my guts
& now you stand here
Write my pain off
an unworkable experience
Bitch!
i want to scream—
& the words—
—unreal
from my mouth
i love you—
i hope you'll be happy.

CHERYL CLARKE

what goes around comes around
or the proof is in the pudding

Truthfulness, honor, is not something which springs ablaze of itself; it has
to be created between people. . . .
ADRIENNE RICH, "Women and Honor"

A woman in my shower crying.
All I can do is make potato salad
and wish I hadn't been caught lying.

I dust the chicken for frying
pretending my real feelings too much a challenge
to the woman in my shower crying.

I forget to boil the eggs, time is flying,
my feet are tired, my nerves frazzled,
and I wish I hadn't been caught lying.

Secondary relationships are trying.
I'd rather roll dough than be hassled
by women in my shower crying.

Truth is clarifying.
Pity it's not more like butter.
I wish I hadn't been caught lying.

Ain't no point denying,
my soufflé won't even flutter.
I withhold from the woman in my shower crying
afraid of the void I filled with lying.

GLORIA ANZALDÚA
Nightvoice

When we met I fell
into her eyes
like falling into warm rock
blurting

everything how my cousins
took turns at night
when I was five eight ten

her eyes asked for nothing
but I turned myself inside
out plucked my heart
and offered it to her.
She looked away

I hated the coaxing in my voice
that bitch whine
and then she said *bueno* just

this once

    It rained hard that day and afterwards
    she sat up and stretched
    arms and bare back glistening.
    The sounds of the *ranas*
    entered the room with the night
    both were drowning her.

I stood at the door
of the heaven I thought out of reach
When I touched her I could barely
breathe and the smell of her:

toasted almonds and yeast.
I could never get near it enough
the wanting making my arms weak

the taste of her
even now if I bring my fingers up to my nose
I get a whiff of her.

    Lightning scored the windowpanes
    a brutal light hit my eyes
    filling the room   surprising
    the shun in her face
    she slid it back behind her eyes
    but I'd seen it
    and by the time thunder
    shook the mirror
    something else had entered the room
    and I knew she would leave me
    parts of her were walking out
    into the *llovizna*
    toward the lightning piercing the horizon

She lay   beached
on the white sand
and before the sweat dried on her body
I knew she needn't

have done anything
one stroke
of her hand on my belly

and I would have gone off again
but I lay on the white sheet
mouth full of sand
my face shut like a door.

    Somehow the thunder had gotten inside me
    and I wanted to say I'm not your *perra*
    a cheap shot but it would have
    softened her mouth
    by then I wanted nothing from her
    had turned away and lay listening
    to the rain and the frogs.
    The birds had stopped singing.

When her hand touched me
I almost screamed.
I pulled back into my self

made myself numb
but the cat her hand found me
and I the mouse had no more

holes to hide in
I came to lose myself
and for that I never

forgave her.

bueno: all right
ranas: frogs
llovizna: rain
perra: bitch as in female dog

JACQUELINE LAPIDUS

Love Is Not One of Those Countries Where You Can Be Sure of the Weather

the storm that broke last weekend
over Brittany where you were
staying with another woman
the gale that wrecked ships
the rain that flooded towns
and washed them out to sea
that torrent in the west
that howl of pain
was me
wanting you back
wishing you drowned
watching hope drip out of me like blood
declaring myself a disaster area

PAMELA SNEED
Jealousy

Nothing prepared me
for the way she smiled at you . . .

In a totally unfeministic fantasy
I want to rip her apart
piece
      by
           piece
be a diva drag queen like
Alexis Carrington and tell her
YOU HAVE TOTALLY OVERSTEPPED YOUR BOUNDS
as I withdraw my claws
recover my face and
pretend
you are a woman I loved
a long time ago.

JAN FREEMAN
That Fallacy

Where is the home when the home is heart
and the heart is divided between two bodies?
Heart divided, lust and love;
heart divided, kiss me, feed me.
Whose home is mine in the morning, love,
when the pillow creases and the neck bends sleep;
when one hand begs here, and the other, touch me;
when one leg folds dream and the other, brace me?
Where is my home when longing breaks me:
one body teases, one body weeps;
when one mouth whispers and one mouth speaks
in normal tones of the home's demise?
Turn, slap the ground, spin, rise above, twist, listen

lovely face, listen solemn face,
I am moving in two directions at once
with nowhere to rest, with no room for sleep,
with no heart at peace; whose hands are peace
to fold around my head, my heart divided?
Shelter is a solid heart; shelter lost, whose home my home
as I move forward, then glance backward, turn around, retrace my steps?
What link, whose skin? My skin is tender; who calls tenderness a
    solid form?
Whose eyes my floor and roof? Whose back a desk, a bed, a kitchen table?

BECKY BIRTHA

Expectations

sometimes it's worse than
    open fighting
the way nothing is special
    anymore

we don't decide to go out
    until the last minute
don't bother to get dressed up
    for each other

you don't want
    sex
and we agree
    to release that expectation

you still want
    to sleep with me, still
    hold me in your sleep
but I wonder for how much longer

in the morning you never
    reach for me
    or smile first

I get less and less
    from you
but keep trying
    to lower my ideals

and I want
    to stay with you
I want
    to feel loved
I want
    to go on giving
    whatever it takes
    from me.

KARLA E. ROSALES

Erotic Reflection IX

TRANSLATED BY CARMEN CHAVEZ

Mujer
estraño el toque conocido
de tus manos fuertes
sobre mi piel
acariciandome

Mujer
recuerdo las noches de tequila
mi cuerpo
la sal
que tu lengua buscaba

Mujer
tengo tu imagen
pintado sobre mi ser.

Woman
I miss that familiar touch
your strong hands
caressing my skin

Woman
I remember nights
filled with tequila
your tongue
in search of my salt
my body

Woman
your image
is painted
in my soul.

JANICE GOULD
Tanana Valley

I spend the summer singing for you
the long walk into town
these hot mornings in Alaska.
The Tanana valley stretches
a hundred miles south
and there tremendous mountains
gleam white with snow.
Along the road fireweed burns,
bumblebees buzz in clover,
someone cuts and bales
a twelve-acre field of hay.

Sometimes in the afternoon
clouds push in over the hills,
the sky darkens, and my body
steams with sweat.
Mosquitos swarm from the dust in the road
and settle in my hair.

I watch the wild rose blossom
and the rose hip bud.
High-bush cranberries ripen
and soon the smoky hue of blueberries
will cover the muskeg bogs.

Every day my thoughts cross Canada
looking for you. Every day I wait
for your letter that never comes.

KATE RUSHIN
A Northern Ohio Love Poem

We spent that winter talking about spring
About how good it would feel
To kick off boots and fly kites

It didn't happen
We never did get over that heavy wool and grey
That ridiculous irritation being mad at the wind

You must've been suffocating
Your long legs jammed into those winter rooms
Full of my friends

You never said   I never asked
Now this winter I hear you've gotten crazy and pitiful
This winter they're saying the same thing about me.

CHERYL CLARKE
Prayer

Why can't I want you?
(Or is it you who don't want me?)
Are you gone again?
Or is it me gone?

No rush of feeling
in that formidable place of violet sentinels
when I open my eyes.

Two years ago
you gave me a sign
to pull back from pretenders.
I'm still pulling
and so are they.

But can we be friends?
Is there no rush of feeling
nor vague chance
we might meet each other again
in that formidable place?

OLGA BROUMAS

Bitterness

*She who loves roses must be patient
and not cry out when she is pierced by thorns.*

SAPPHO

In parody
of a grade B film, our private
self-conscious soapie, as we fall
into the common, suspended disbelief of love, you ask
will I still be
here tomorrow, next week, tonight you ask am I really
here. My passion delights

and surprises you, comfortable
as you've been without it. Lulled
comfortable as a float myself in your real
and rounded arms, I can only smile
back, indulgently
at such questions. In the second reel—

a season of weeks, two
flights across the glamorous Atlantic, one
orgy and the predictable divorce
scenes later—I'm fading out
in the final close-up
alone. As one

heroine of this
two-bit production to the other, how long

did you, did we both know
the script
meant you to wake up doubting
in those first nights, not me, my daytime
serial solvency, but yours.

AUDRE LORDE
Parting

Belligerent and beautiful as a trapped ibis
your lean hands are a sacrifice
spoken three times
before dawn
there is blood in the morning egg
that makes me turn and weep
I see you
weaving pain into garlands
the shape of a noose
while I grow
weary
of licking my heart
for moisture
cactus tongued.

ROBIN MORGAN
From Ten Sonnets to the Light Lady
VII. Dreaming the Volcano

Barefoot on steaming ash I climbed toward you,
unhurried, unscorched: this was our element.
Behind me, sudden cinquefoil slate blue
lupine sprang and flowered in each footprint.

We had been warned, you and I, about this place:
volatile, steep, erupting ancient geysers,
sulfurine, fountaining fiery lace.
The scarp itself was sintered with dead lovers.
But we met as always at the appointed crater,
laughing, eyes blazing as we leapt the crust,
twin plumes of lava coursing through each other,
to arc, flame, flow in sacred lust.
Then, safe in your smoldering arms, I slept,
at peace. And woke in bed, alone. And wept.

IRENA KLEPFISZ

periods of stress

it is unwise during periods of stress
or change to formulate new theories
case in point: when about to begin
a new love affair   without having ended
the previous one   do not maintain
that more freedom is required for the full expression
of individual personality   or that various
life styles are possible   and all kinds of interesting
situations   still need to be explored.

try instead: i am tired   tired
of the nearness   this small apartment
of the watering can and level of the window
shade.   i prefer to drift towards more spacious rooms
towards intimate restaurants and dimly lit unfamiliar
beds   new love techniques.   but
do not throw me out.   i am too
frightened to venture out alone.
let me stay till i'm secure again
somewhere else   and then leave me alone.

JUDY GRAHN
If you lose your lover

If you lose your lover
rain hurt you. blackbirds
brood over the sky trees
burn down everywhere brown
rabbits run under
car wheels. should your
body cry? to feel such
blue and empty bed dont
bother. if you lose your
lover comb hair go here
or there get   another

ELENA GEORGIOU
An Interracial Relationship and A Window

never fall
in love with someone
who lives in your building
because when it's over the window
from which you once blew each other
goodbye kisses transforms into a window
from which you pretend to be daydreaming
when you're really waiting to see
if her body's changed
if her hair's grown
and if she leaves before
you do so you can
walk without fear
of bumping into a love killed
because no word
no gesture and

nobody goes unscrutinized
in a relationship
when one person is   white
the other black
in america

MARY ANN MCFADDEN
After the Crash the Old Fool Does Laundry

It's given now. We've only to live it through, gracefully, I trust,
accepting these wintry mishaps for what they are.
The blouse blown against the fence is not a curse on us,
although it irritates us just as though it were.
And if you find me odd, and old, and even, therefore,
faintly disgusting, I find you callow, difficult to bear.
We are less indestructible than we at first appeared.
I belong to my desk and my dishevelled floors,
to this droll celibacy, to the task of living alone here,
though not utterly chosen nor altogether enforced,
more than I belong to you, who have come to my voice
as lover and nightmare, and who will be taken away,
not thank God by car crash, but daily as I make my bed,
sheets rinsed of event, and of memory.

LISA VICE
Water Cupped In My Hands

We sit together under blue umbrellas
drinking cappuccino and sambuca
even though it is all over
I unbuckle my sandals and you rub my cold feet.

You tell me a story of a doll you once loved so much
you breathed life into her soft rubber body
ran with her in your dreams till one day with no warning
you bit off the fingertips of her left hand.

Knee to knee in the mist of rain
we laugh as the waitress rushes to gather paper lanterns
we never speak of the lateness
or your long trip back to Greenpoint.

You come home with me
even though it is all over
let me carry you through the night like water
cupped in my hands.

With your damp head resting under my chin
I learn by heart
the way moonlight changes to sunlight
on the mimosa trees.

JACQUELINE LAPIDUS
Healing

after each quarrel I
rush into the bedroom
for a good cry
so hard to comfort myself
without the sea nearby
I need sheets and blankets
and curtains the color
of a Greek sky in summer
and a bluegreen carpet lapping
at my feet

after each quarrel I
avoid mirrors, seek

friendly faces around me
how can I love myself
without other women   three
nudes on the wall, rubbing
their sepia bodies warm from the bath
and winged Isis gazing
into a twin sister's eyes

after each quarrel she
collapses   her mouth closes
like a flower choking down a bee

ashamed of my stinging words
I read poems   write poems
healing myself
for overtures   my toes
against her toes
my breasts brushing her back
her name like a wafer on my tongue

MAY SWENSON
Poet to Tiger

The Hair

You went downstairs
saw a hair in the sink
and squeezed my toothpaste by the neck.
You roared. My ribs are sore.
This morning even my pencil's got your toothmarks.
Big Cat Eye cocked on me you see bird bones.
Snuggled in the rug of your belly
your breath so warm
I smell delicious fear.
Come breathe on me rough pard
put soft paws here.

The Salt

You don't put salt on anything
so I'm eating without.
Honey on the eggs is all right
mustard on the toast.
I'm not complaining I'm saying I'm
living with *you*.
You like your meat raw
don't care if it's cold.
Your stomach must have tastebuds
you swallow so fast.
Night falls early. It's foggy. Just now

I found another of your bite marks in the cheese.
I'm hungry. Please
come bounding home
I'll hand you the wine to open
with your teeth.
Scorch me a steak unsalted
boil my coffee twice
say the blessing to a jingle on the blue TV.
Under the lap robe on our chilly couch
look behind my ears "for welps"
and hug me.

The Sand

You're right I brought a grain
or two of sand
into bed I guess in my socks.
But it was you pushed them off
along with everything else.

Asleep you flip
over roll
everything under
you and off

me. I'm always grabbing
for my share of the sheets.

Or else you wake me every hour with sudden
growled I-love-yous
trapping my face between those plushy
shoulders. All my float-dreams turn spins
and never finish. I'm thinner
now. My watch keeps running fast.
But best is when we're riding pillion
my hips within your lap. You let me steer.
Your hand and arm go clear
around my ribs your moist
dream teeth fastened on my nape.

A grain of sand in the bed upsets you or
a hair on the floor.
But you'll get
in slick and wet from the shower if I let
you. Or with your wool cap
and skiing jacket on
if it's cold.
Tiger don't scold me
don't make me comb my hair outdoors.

Cuff me careful. Lick don't
crunch. Make last what's yours.

The Dream

You get into the tub holding *The Naked Ape*
in your teeth. You wet that blond
three-cornered pelt lie back wide
chest afloat. You're reading
in the rising steam and I'm
drinking coffee from your tiger cup.
You say you dreamed
I had your baby book

and it was pink and blue.
I pointed to a page and there
was your face with a cub grin.

You put your paws in your armpits
make a tiger-moo.
Then you say: "Come here
Poet and take
this hair
off me." I do.
It's one of mine. I carefully
kill it and carry
it outside. And stamp on it
and bury it.

In the begonia bed.
And then take off my shoes
not to bring a grain
of sand in to get
into our bed.
I'm going to
do the cooking
now instead
of you.
And sneak some salt in
when you're not looking.

MINNIE BRUCE PRATT
Staying Together

Do you know why I think we stay together?

Because we fight in the car on the Beltway,
first about doing our clothes in a Rockville laundrymat,
then about everything: closeness, farness, love;
you mad enough to drive into an abutment,
me mad enough to open my door and jump;
both yelling, crying, past the Mormon Temple
lit like a Disney spaceship, which makes me
feel worse, like we're on the wrong planet.

After we both say, in different, loud frenzy:
How can anything be worth this? silence for twenty
minutes, the brief repeated glare of mile markers.
Then you ask in a mouselike voice if I would like
to go get in a hot tub with you, and I laugh.

THE
ENDURANCE/
EVOLUTION/
ECSTASY OF LOVE

Sandra Monroe and Sandra Goings, Michigan Womyn's Music Festival, 1994
(Joyce Culver)

TRUST
AND
HAVEN

Do you think I'll ever make it to 'E'?" my poet friend asked. "Who cares about 'E'?" a single friend scoffed. "I hate the idea of working hard on a relationship. I know it's a sterling thing to have, but for me: Move on. I always liked what came next. One of the wonderful things about gay life is that you stay friends. You see them go on to better things too. I like my independence and my friends." This is one choice along the arc of love.

But you don't have to be part of a couple to make it to "E." Endurance/Evolution/Ecstasy can also mean reaching that point in life where you like who you are and where you are going—with or without a partner. Bravely we have built a great visible lesbian and gay community, extensively organized to offer services, culture, activism, camaraderie.

Most couples consider endurance in terms of commitment—the enduring nature of passionate long-lasting love. What are the special values of staying together? From the direction of the heart: We bring out the best in each other. We actively support the best for each other. This gives us the freedom to change and reach out in new ways. A bedrock of trust is established, yet we don't take each other for granted. Fulfilling lusty appetites deepens gloriously and gorgeously. Sex becomes sacred. Flare-ups are given time and space to dampen down. Playfulness and laughter are ever welcome as the art of negotiation is continually practiced and improved upon.

Muriel Rukeyser's "Anemone" is an incantation to the mysteries of love and existence.

My sex is closing, my sex is opening.
You are singing and offering: the way in.

My life is closing, my life is opening.
You are here.

For some women the struggle is worth it, and the struggles can include physical and life-challenging realities. Jane Chambers, dying from cancer, watches over ". . . Beth On Her Forty-second Birthday" as she sleeps through the night.

> *Swathed in my childhood*
> *quilt, where so many of my childhood dreams*
> *were born, most of which you have made come*
> *true.*

Evolution refers to the adventurous path love requires. Earlier this century Gertrude Stein and Alice B. Toklas trailblazed their way into classic lesbian couplehood, even though at the time we could never be sure. Stein's writings, which affirmed her love, were not published until long after her death.

> *She is that kind of a wife.   She can see.*
> *And a credit to me.*
> . . . .
> *capridinks is pretty and winks, winks of sleep and winks of love.*
> *Capridinks.   Capridinks is my love and my Coney.*

The fragility of each day as we age is captured when Naomi Replansky sees her lover cross the city street.

> *Then suddenly I feared the cars,*
> *The streets you cross, the days you pass.*
> *You hold me as a glass holds water.*
> *You can be shattered like a glass.*

Gale Jackson celebrates "an anniversary of sorts: the seventeenth of july":

> *where the explosion of a star lifetimes ago*
> *is visible now in your eyes climbing into me*
> *you resting in the arms of a hunger older than we*
> *could ever know*

Joyful relationships that live and breathe and change over time are infused with ecstasy.

Victoria Lena Manyarrows remembers when:

> our kisses were waterfalls
> and the Indian women, our ancestors
> drenched us with tears, their joy and
> sadness flowing like rivers . . .

Ecstasy involves compelling elements: the capacity to see beauty in nature, the privilege of chosen satisfying work, the stimulation of abiding interests and friends, the exultation of passion and desire between women in love.

Free of society's prescriptions of how to be, two women together continually invent new ways of being. With imagination and perception our poets communicate the transformative and energizing power of love.

SAPPHO

The gods bless you

May you sleep then
on some tender
girl friend's breast

CHRYSTOS
A Soft Indentation

in my body where yours slept around me
like the gold grass hollow
deer leave in the morning meadow
or the curve of a whale rib

beached on the rocks
I carried back to admire
along the path to my door
A tenderness is yours I feel for
the mountain which centers my life
We are wary of old words used
to describe these circles
We awaken at dawn   leave each other dreaming
slip into the wild edge where reason fails
your branches shelter
mine flower

MICHELLE CLIFF
And What Would It Be Like

And what would it be like
The terrain of my girlhood

[with you]?   There is no map

Ok.
mangoes
then the sweet liquidity of star apple
custard apple
sweetsop
cut with sharp tamarind
washed down with coconut water
ginep   slippery
papaya
where restless baby-ghosts vent their furies

all devoured
against trade winds
                    Will I eternally return to the Trade?

Then—

there's more
by which I mean
hibiscus, jasmine, night-blooming   and otherwise
by which I mean
the more ancient
pre-Columbian   pre-Contact
growth
edenic underbrush
unyielding   thick as a woman's thatch
like the [girl's school legend] un-drawered tennis mistress
who
or whom
we slid beneath
to glimpse the bright, thick ginger
womanly—
God, we wanted to be women, never knowing what that meant.
—patch
thatch so thick you'd never guess she was British
our prejudice.

And banana leaves
which are as wide as a girl's waist—sometimes
and as long as a girl's feathered legs
which exude the juice of the fruit
without a taste of the fruit
dependable as any aunt

down a falls once owned by an aunt
we flowed
on the impossible green
into the equally impossible blue
lit by the height of an impossible light
taking our half-naked selves
down the sweet
into the salt
water
and women
women and water
my grandmother's river
my distant aunt's falls

no one else was allowed in
children   that didn't feel right
revolutionaries are made, not born.

II

Bougainvillea
grows
[in the botanist's term]
in showy profusion—
but scentless—
disappoints.

III

Under the high-leggéd mahogany bed
caciques at each corner   like apostles
the tail of a scorpion is set to strike
transparent   dangerous
I know its poison.

IV

All feels wild from this distance.

V

Once at Cable Hut
I fell into a sinkhole
down and down and down
but came back up
Once I had my period and swam way out
past the coral reef
and wondered if a shark would be drawn to me
as the warm salt drew the blood out   and the sea roared
Once I speared a lobster clean   underwater at Lime Key

Once I brushed beside the flimsy nightdress
of a jellyfish   and have a mark on my leg to prove it
Once I dodged an alligator in a swamp at the Carib's edge
my mouth gorged on a hundred oysters   their grit becoming
pearl against my teeth
Once I played with a cousin's cock underwater
he taught me to shoot coconuts between the eyes so they
rained
on the sand   it was the least I could do
Those were the dangerous days
There was nothing to stop us   it seemed

VI

There is no map
only the most ragged path back   to
my love   so much so
she ended up in the bush
                    at a school where such things were
taken very seriously   severely
                    and
I was left   missing her   never ceasing
                    and
she was watched   for signs
                    and
I was left   alone   missing her   never ceasing
                    and
she was not allowed to write   at least she never did
                    and
I walked the length and breadth of the playing fields
                    I have never felt so lost
not like that
                    and
I wanted to be dead   that's all
                                        finally
the headmistress and head girl found me
in the stacks
                    weeping
                                        violently

against spines of biology
                        running into history
I can see myself in the lapsed documentary of memory
                        curled up against books, shelves
salting the sea island cotton of my blouse
                    water tearing down my face, school badge
with cross & crown   & Latin motto
                  my parents were summoned
the word was not spoken
                      I was told to forget everything
I would never see her again   I would never see her again
           except in my mind   and to this day
golden
              they rifled my hiding place
ransacked my words   read me aloud   on the
verandah
            in the impossible sun
my father   uttering
"When you're twenty we'll laugh about this."
            that I remember
they took me, on the advice of the doctor who delivered
me,
            to Doctor's Cave,
which is a beach, not Prospero's vault,
            for weeks
I swam
            like Caliban
her feathered legs opening underwater   salt rushing in
            I was exhausted, they said
excitable

I wanted to be a wild colonial girl
And for a time, I was.

ROBIN BECKER
Midnight Swim

She likes the comely shape of the copper beech
and notes the wedge of sky that shows where the tree
received stigmata.   I like to watch her
walk up the path because she is beautiful and
sees beauty where I see sadness: in the retreating summer
night, in the night of the pond's enormous, still eye,
in the amphitheater of bullfrog and treefrog and peeper,
in the silver steam coming off the water, in the arc
of the diving body disappearing, in the splash of a creature
nearing we name turtle or snake. The floating dock
drifts with its jealous reflection appearing like a face.
And I who have no claim on this woman or this lake
take the measure of the summer from the fireflies—
luminous against the dark trees—and the slowly revolving
dock I dream free of its moorings by morning.

VICTORIA LENA MANYARROWS
Ribbon Women

woman, native woman
  colors wrap around you, ribbon woman
  as the wind blows your ribbons and hair
  into a tangle of colours and love

around you the drumbeat's rising
  bringing you back to the land of your birth
  carrying you home and away
    from the white man's lies
your heart is pounding

I remember when
  you embraced me then

at the pow wow we were young
and the music of men was near
our kisses were waterfalls
and the Indian women, our ancestors
drenched us with tears, their joy and
　　　　　sadness flowing like rivers flooded
past woodlands and open prairies

they remembered our love
they believed in our love

they hold us now, wanting us
　　　　to continue our touches
our ribbons flowing
　　　　entangled together
lips pressing lips in the fire of the moment

if the drums should draw us apart
and the winds should separate us
　　　don't be sad
we will be joined again
　　　and the moonlight will remember our love

ELIZABETH CLARE

East Oakland

Old photographs: your hair
straight, parted, curled
at the ends. Mouth tight,
eyes refuse the camera.
I wouldn't have
recognized you then

and now you lean against
the door frame laughing, short
short afro, broad smile.

East Oakland, 1965:
your brothers in and out
of jail, gun fights down
the street, and every morning
your mama straightened your hair,
burning the back of your neck.

You tip your chair back,
hands crossed behind head,
watch your reflection
in the night-black window.
You say *my daddy
always sits like this.*

I want to dance, want
your hand light
on the small
of my back, want
our bodies to catch
the rhythm: words
never ceasing.

You write:
*At first
we held hands
like children
who bravely choose partners.*

Then tell me: *my second year
of college I took a field trip, busload
of white kids and me. We drove down
96th Avenue, right past the house
I grew up in, its square yard. Home
called ghetto for the first time.*

And me: that white town
I call home. North
of Bald Mountain they say
there is a lynching tree, just follow
the logging roads.

The tremors of my
cerebral palsy reach
through the arc of our walk,
hands swing into the rhythm,
your palm cool and dry,
subway to 54th Street.
Words never ceasing.

They taunted me *weirdo, retard,*
monkey, hey lezzie. Taunted you—
you don't say the words. I spread
my body quiet against yours,
try to imagine East Oakland, 1965.

Later we walk to your car,
the night, crisp quiet
urban dark, I steady my hand
in yours, count the tremors.

NAOMI REPLANSKY

The Dangerous World

I watched you walk across the street,
Slightly stooped, not seeing me,
And smiled to see that mixture of
Clumsiness, grace, intensity.

Then suddenly I feared the cars,
The streets you cross, the days you pass.
You hold me as a glass holds water.
You can be shattered like a glass.

MINNIE BRUCE PRATT

Shame

1.
I ask for justice but do not release
myself.   Do I think I was wrong?   Yes.
Of course.   Was wrong.   Am wrong.   Can
justify everything except their pain.
Even now their cries rattle in my ears
like icy winds pierce in cold weather.
Even now a tenderness from their cries.

The past repeats in fragments: What I
see is everybody watching, me included,
as a selfish woman leaves her children,
two small boys hardly more than babies.

Though I say he took them, and my theories
explain power, how he thought he'd force
me to choose, me or them, her or them.

2.
How I wanted her slant humid body,
that first woman, silent reach,
how I began with her furtive mouth,
her silences, her hand fucking me
back of the van, beach sand grit
scritch at my jeans, low tide.

The boys yelling in myrtle thickets
outside, hurl pell-mell, count hide-
and-seek.   The youngest opens the door.
What I am doing is escape into clouds,
grey heat, promise of thunderstorm
not ominous, not sordid, from ground
to air, like us flying kites in March.
But here it's July and I'm doing what?

Curious, left out, he tells some fragment later
to the father, who already knows.   The threats
get worse, spat curses: He'll take the children;
I can go fly where I damn please in the world.
The muttered words for scum, something rotten,
flies buzzing, futile, mean.

                              If I had been
more ashamed, if I had not wanted the world.
If I had hid my lust, I might not have lost
them.   This is where the shame starts.

If I had not been so starved, if I had been
more ashamed and hid.   No end to this blame.

3.
At times I can say it was good, even better
for them, my hunger for her.   Now that we're
here, they've grown up, survived, no suicides,
despite their talk of walks in front of cars,
smashing through plate glass.   Despite guilt:

        The long sweating calls to the twelve-year-
        old, saying, *Hold on* against the pain,
        how I knew it from when I left, the blame
        inside, the splintered self, saying to him, *Walk
        out,* remind the body you are alive, even if
        rain is freezing in the thickets to clatter
        like icy seeds, even if you are the only one
        plodding through the drifts of grainy snow.

Now we've survived.   They call to talk poetry
or chaos of physics.   Out of the blue to hear
their voices, a kind of forgiveness, a giddy
lifting of my heart:

                    Like the kites we flew once
        below the Occoneechee Mountain, down in the pasture.
        The wind spirited our plastic birds, hawks, eagles,
        or crumpled them while we shouted, *No, no.*   I waded

deep into the blackberry thicket thorns for the miracle
wings that soon we made disappear again like airplanes,
soon made to come back from mystery travels:

The way the boys appear today in my city, old enough to
come by rackety plane or train, whiz in to be
with me, my lover now, eat spaghetti, talk serious
politics in my kitchen, snug, but a feeling of travel.
Their curious eyes are on life that widens in a place
little known, our pleasure without shame.   We talk
and the walls seem to shift and expand around us.
The breaking of some frozen frame.   The youngest jokes
lovebirds at our held hands.   Late evening we stir.
Goodnight: they expect me to go off to bed with her.

4.
All the years between now and then, the nights.
One December when I thought she would leave me,
was weeping her hand's loss, her body's weight

lifting away, and thought: I will lose her
like I lost the children.   I will lose her.
And knew my body's secret thought, endured

as a voice creeping on my skin, a buzz,
a sandfly's bite of pain, a grain of sand
caught in the sheets, abrading my skin.   *Loss,*

said the voice, *love is loss.*   Don't forget
the children, how pleasure brings pain.
Don't forget you're to blame.   Don't forget

how pain digs in your hands, like thorns stuck
and broken off, invisible ache you feel
whenever you touch.   You lose what you touch.

You've learned it.   Don't want too much.
Think of her arms as nothing: blowing foam,
drifting cloud, scudding caress.

Reality is flesh of your flesh taken.
What you want to last is fantasy, imagination,
said the voice creeping in my body, pain.

5.
In one hand, the memory of pain.
I reread one of these poems and begin
again (again, it's been fifteen years)
to cry at the fragmented naked faces,
at the noise of the crying, somewhere
inside us, even now, like an old wind.
In one hand, the memory of pain.

In the other hand, change.   When
did it begin? Over and over.   Once
we all were walking on the street,
me and her, hand in hand, very loud
singing sixties rock-and-roll, rattle,
shake, smiling goofily, indecent
(but not quite illegally), escaped
out with the boys in a gusty wind.
The youngest sang, the oldest lagged,
ashamed?   But we waited for him.
It was a comedy, a happy ending,
pleasure.   We kept saying, *Spring,*
it's spring, so the boys brought us
to their lake, its body-thick ice thinned
at the edge to broken glass splinters.
The new waves widened and glittered in the ice,
a delicate clinking like glass wind chimes.

And now, sometimes, one of them will say: *Remember*
the day we all went down to the lake?   Remember
how we heard the sound of the last ice in the water?

OLGA BROUMAS
Four Beginnings/for Kyra

1. You raise
   your face from mine, parting
   my breath like water, hair falling
   away in its own wind, and your eyes—
   green in the light like honey—surfacing
   on my body, awed
   with desire, speechless, this common dream.

2. You bore your marriage like a misconceived
   animal, and have the scars, the pale
   ridged tissue round front and back
   for proof.   For proof.   Tonight

   we cross into each other's language.   I take your hand
   hesitant still with regret
   into that milky landscape, where braille
   is a tongue for lovers, where tongue,
   fingers, lips
   share a lidless eye.

3. I was surprised myself—the image of the lithe
   hermaphroditic lover a staple of
   every fantasy, bought, borrowed, or mine.   We never did
   mention the word, unqualified: I love:
   your hair, I love: your feet, toes, tender nibbles, I love:

   I love. You are the memory
   of each desire that ran, dead-end, into a mind
   programmed to misconstrue it.   A mind inventing
   neurosis, anxiety, phobia, a mind expertly camouflaged
   from the thought of love
   for a woman, its native
   love.

4. I in my narrow body, spellbound
   against your flesh.

SUZANNE GARDINIER
Fishing Trip

The blues were running and your mouth dangerous
and sweet after lemonade at the Knights
of Columbus carnival, where girls I grew up with
wheeled babies past the amateur hawkers
and packs of fathers played roulette and drank.
We kissed in the parking lot, protected only

by out-of-state plates and a full gas tank,
then escaped with rented tackle in the trunk
to fish the flood tides from the outer beaches.
Some fishermen worked three rods at a time
with sandspikes and torches almost in the surf
and an old guy who used to be harbormaster
told about the blues' teeth and their fight,

how one tailwalked the waves just before we arrived.
We baited with sea worms, cast into the churn
and hardly grappled half an hour
before our grips tired and we'd hauled enough,
slit, gutted, and iced in the cooler,
for a week of suppers. From the sand spit

I could see the faint circle of Ferris-wheel lights
on and off, as mist sucked in and out of the harbor,
and you put your hands under my clothes,
away from the torches, hungry. We headed
for the car, the city, bed. The stacked fish
shifted in the cooler between us
and we staggered under the weight of abundance.

MARGARET ROBISON
Gold

I woke grieving for my paralyzed leg
with its memories of October walks, grieving
for my paralyzed arm and hand
with their own longings and hopes.
I *will* recover from this stroke,
I tell myself, but fear
lies like lead in my belly
and I look for images
to string together like prayer beads
against despair: wrens
at the feeder, flame
of sumac, evergreens. And making love
in the woods that fall when, for awhile,
everything felt possible, the ground thick
with leaves. So gold.
So gold.

MARGARET ROBISON
I Opened My Hand

I'm startled awake nights
by the touch of my paralyzed hand on my face.
And I read in a book about healing
that a single strand of DNA holds
the history of the universe.
I keep trying to remember how it felt
before it went numb, the feel
of your nipple under my thumb.
Or my fingers, how they would open
with such apparent ease, like the time
you gave me a stone
and I opened my hand, not knowing
that acceptance
would bind me to you forever.

PAT PARKER

From Love Poems

Let me come to you naked
come without my masks
come dark
     and lay beside you

Let me come to you old
come as a dying snail
come weak
     and lay beside you

Let me come to you angry
come shaking with hate
come callused
     and lay beside you

even more

Let me come to you strong
come sure and free
come powerful

and lay with you

MERLE WOO

Untitled

In the deepest night and a full moon,
at once riding the flying mare and being her
my own pumping broad wings, ascending higher—

My legs around that great horse's neck
not riding
but my body singing down under
in front of the beautiful dark head

feeling her moist tongue in my center—
I am risking my life for these moments,
My head possibly dashed against the rocks.

Now riding with our rhythms matching,
the exertion of her back's muscles and
the mounting pulsations between my thighs—

Higher and soaring through mist and above mountains
shaped like jagged spires
the cold thin air ripping through my lungs—

We finish.
And you lay your head on my thigh,
your wings enfolding my legs, and we rest.

GALE JACKSON

an anniversary of sorts:
the seventeenth of july

slowly
on foot from a million miles apart
and this whole year towards me you we
enter so wild and gentle the underbelly
of magic where seals sing deep under the sea
where the explosion of a star lifetimes ago
is visible now in your eyes climbing into me
you resting in the arms of a hunger older than we
could ever know who have come so slow by foot and life
to this place where an ocean waits inside of us.

GERTRUDE STEIN

From A Sonatina Followed By Another

She is that kind of a wife. She can see.
  And a credit to me.
  And a credit to me she is sleepily a credit to me and what do I credit
her with I credit her with a kiss.
    1. Always sweet.
    2. Always right.
    3. Always welcome.
    4. Always wife.
    5. Always blessed.
    6. Always a successful druggist of the second class and we
know what that means. Who credits her with all this a husband with a
kiss and what is he to be always more lovingly his missus' help and
hero. And when is he heroic, well we know when.
  Win on a foul pretty as an owl pretty as an owl win on a fowl. And
the fowl is me and she is pretty as an owl. Battling Siki and Capridinks
capridinks is pretty and winks, winks of sleep and winks of love.
Capridinks. Capridinks is my love and my Coney.

MINNIE BRUCE PRATT
Husband

The man sitting next to me on the grass at the March on Washington
asks, "Is he your husband?" as I return from kissing you, as you step
down from the microphone. On stage, a drag queen in beaded white
chiffon is ferociously lip-synching and tail-switching an answer to the
introduction you have given her, praise from a drag king resplendent in
your black-on-black suit. In the audience, I hesitate over my answer. Do
I change the pronoun *and* the designation of *husband*? Finally I reply,
"Yes, she is." He hesitates in his turn: "He hasn't gone through the oper-
ation?" The complexity of your history crowds around me as I mentally
juggle your female birth sex, male gender expression. I say, "She's trans-
gendered, not transsexual." Up on stage Miss Liberty is reading, with
sexy histrionics and flourishs of her enormous torch, a proclamation

from a woman who is a U.S. senator, a speech that trumpets and drums with the cadences of civil rights. The man blinks his eyelashes flirtatiously, leans toward me, whiskey on his breath, waves his hand at his companions, "We're up from North Carolina." Then, femme to femme, he begins to talk of your beauty: "He is perfect. If I ever wanted a woman it would be someone just like her." With innuendo and arch look he gives truthful ambiguity to what he sees in me, in you, something not simply about "gay rights." The queen whispers in my ear with his sharp steaming breath, "Don't let her get away. Hang *on* to him."

ANA SISNETT
Mango Tree Love Song

. . . In the midst of it all
the mangoes grow plentiful,
in bunches,
like grapes hanging
from giant trees.

To stand under a mango tree
is to stand
under a woman's dress.

Her massive trunk:
sturdy legs held together
in defiance of
all that would violate
her existence.

I,
made small and humble
in her presence

heart beating
LOUDER
than thunder

spread my hands
fingertips on fire

TOUCH

spread my arms
around her
and listen to her. . . .

whispers. . . .

listen to her stories
of others gone before me.

I ease my way up carefully

through all her branches

loving her,
slowly, tenderly

until I reach a branch

sturdy enough to
hold the weight
of all
that I carry.

I ease my way along
slowly, tenderly
to its tip

where I,
with her permission,
receive the offering,
her fruit.

I climb down joyfully
hugging her,
covering the full length of her

with my sweat
with my kisses
leaving bits of my flesh
and locks of my hair
tangled in her bark.

When my feet touch the
cool earth again
I press my lips to her roots
and kiss her

in thanksgiving.

PAMELA SNEED

Precious Crazy Girl Giggles

Collard greens blue fish brown rice
Juniors strawberry cheesecake
you are the sweet taste main ingredient
season summer salt cook culinary artist
shake bake swing shuffle and shoo bee dooo waa

Midnight talks on the telephone
my favorite after dinner drink
Ethel Waters' skirt lifting
a serious shake bake swing shuffle and shoo bee dooo waaa

You are magic mommie
conjuring up ancestral spirits
when you swing your head back
and sing
releasing unrestrained laughter
please precious crazy girl giggles
feast for poor eyes
shake shake spin
and kiss
the morning we met.

MAYA ISLAS

From Details of a Violent Saint

45
After Picasso,
a survival guide to my new sincerity.

Drawing through imitation of lines
releases a personal seed inside my neurons,
following the path of light
inside the nerve,
it forms an edge,
brings me closer to the Woman I am,
powerful flesh of softness
recreating the universe,
passing through in utter solitude,
galactic sensual scene between two breasts.

Now,
I know myself,
and my haunting presence.

DOROTHY ALLISON

Dumpling Child

A southern dumpling child
   biscuit eater, tea sipper
   okra slicer, gravy dipper,
I fry my potatoes with onions
   stew my greens with pork

And ride my lover high up
on the butterfat shine of her thighs
where her belly arches and sweetly tastes
of rock salt on watermelon
sunshine sharp teeth bite light
and lick slow like mama's
favorite dumpling child.

JAN FREEMAN
Autumn Sequence

V
I have begun to dream her
hands arms face face fingers mouth
I have begun to dream her love mouth lips
wide lips full wide eyes mouth teeth tongue
I have begun to dream her legs thighs hips
bottom belly I have begun to dream her mouth thighs breasts
belly thighs thighs neck cheeks brows I have begun to dream her
arms hands back hands thighs calves mouth neck breasts
wrists shoulders thighs mouth teeth tongue
I have begun to dream her heart mind mouth hands mind heart
legs arms neck face hair mouth open wider slick grinding into palms
soft slick labia I have begun to dream her hard slick clit fingers on the tip
fingers on the sides swell red clit fingers dipping in fingers over smooth
hole open slightly open wider gently fingers over walls breath blown over
hard clit breath blown slightly into tongue tip barely over hard slick
tongue more firmly over walls into open over base of the hard clit over
    base
of the clit back back into anus open firmly into breath blown lightly
    over tongue
lightly over hard clit tongue fingers deeply deeply tongue flat over
    fingers deep
in open deep in out deeper in out tongue back mouth sucking slowly
    harder sucking
firm clit harder fingers back in out in out slow circles slower one finger
on the anus open one finger slowly circle pointing tongue in the open
    circle slowly
slowly circle tongue moving deeper finger circling wide body lifting
    open wider
legs open wider lips moving gently over slickness over soft slick hard
    slick lightly
lips over fingers lightly fingers lighter tongue slowly tongue slower body
dropping slowly down body slowly legs folding lightly hand down
    slowly down
I have begun to dream her hair over forehead cheeks damp hips rest
    down I have

begun to dream her mouth slowly mouth lips on lips tongue against
   tongue I
have begun to dream her eyes on eyes mouth on mouth hands over
   hands
face against face legs over legs I have begun to dream her stop.

BETH BRANT
Letter From Wolf Pen Road, Kentucky
FOR DENISE

This morning I saw three doe. They stood, confident, alert, delicately foraging on the clover that grows in the meadow. Their ears twitched and they ran off, leaving me to praise them.

It is Sunday and I wonder what you are doing at this hour. Drinking coffee in the back yard by the flowers, pulling weeds, listening for the sound of my voice traveling across the psychic distance to tell you of the sight of Deer that caused my breath to halt, and made me call out—Denise, look!

○

Yesterday I walked across meadow. Rabbit and Groundhog jumped away from my clumsy human stride. Crow yelled at me for walking past his tree. Indigo Bunting flashed by—black, then blue, as the sun touched her feathers. You would have touched me—look, look, did you see it! I would have grabbed your arm—yes, yes!

Flower and herbs bloom in the yard. I picked Russian Sage, Queen Anne's Lace, Tansy, Black-eyed Susan for my studio. They bend gracefully from the clear vase, almost touching the table and Hawk's feather I found a few days ago. Candles are burning. The computer emits a small hum that synchronises with the Bumblebees that fly outside the windows. Ali, the Cat, sleeps behind the computer, in the sunlight.

I am writing again. This small fact in the midst of all this.

○

The other night, I dreamt that you were lying beside me. I reached for you and touched the pillow instead. I awoke and went to the window. The full moon was shining on the corn field. Cicada and Katydid were speaking to the dark. I sat in the chair by the window until dawn, watching the colours of night change to ones of day.

I am missing the sweetness of you, the gentle voice and touch of your love. The conversation and laughter.

It has been hot, humid; the days shimmering with intensity and brightness. There was a storm—the hail and rain caused steam to rise from Earth. After it was over, two fawns came hesitantly to the edge of the corn field, their mother guarding the space they occupied. A distant, left-over crack of lightning sent them back into the woods, the safety of trees quickly hiding their white-spotted cinnamon coats. Mother followed leisurely behind. Robin was taking a bath in a puddle by my studio. He exuberantly splashed, dipping his head into the water, flapping his wings, shaking his body until the water had completely covered him. The grass grew an inch.

I am writing again. A small act in the company of spotted fawns and corn.

9

There is a pond. Trekking across meadow, following the tree line until I heard the croak of frogs. I sat on a small hummock, watching for Turtle; hoping for Blue Heron.
I remembered the time you and I sat at the edge of Lake Erie near the pile of rocks and boulders. Blue Heron seemed to rise up out of the lake, gliding in, her long, thin legs reaching out to the rocks. She was so close, we could hear the great *whoosh* of her wings as she landed. This creature who shows us herself so often; each time, every time, new and glorious, reminding us of possibility, and faith. This life, this love we have chosen and forged to make lasting and beautiful. To make an entity where each of us is whole.

There are Catalpa trees. Long past the time of flowering, their clusters of pods have released the seeds that are scattered in the tall weeds. The Creek call them *Kutuhlpa,* head with wings, after the showy white flowers. Suddenly, there are more Butterflies. Mourningcloak, Viceroy,

Monarch, Zebra Swallowtail. They came in abundance after the rains, moving from Phlox to Bee Balm to Mallow. They flit past my window as Ali and I watch.

Oh, my love, can you see them? Does my wonder and thankfulness transport these gifts to you? Denise, look! Denise, listen! Denise. Denise.

○

I am writing again. This small and simple act in the presence of Earth's abundant magic.
Each morning I walk to my studio, words forming in my mind, on my lips. Words hover on the mist, hang from the corn tassels, float on the hooves of fawns. Words grow from the soil, fly on Cuckoo's wing, move on the breath of Sweetgrass I burn at my desk. At night, words brush against my sleep, like Fireflies in my mind.
Today, I walked to the corn field, put my face to the stalk, felt the sharp greenness against my cheek.
Today, I looked up and saw Heron before she veered off into the trees. Denise, look!

Today, I write these words and know that you will feel them in the dream time before wakefulness. Will see them in the lush array of our years together. Will touch them as you bend to pick the roses that will welcome me home again.

JANE CHAMBERS

To Beth On Her Forty-second Birthday

I sat up all night and watched you sleep. I did,
all night. At midnight you became a year older
but you didn't know it. Swathed in my childhood
quilt, where so many of my childhood dreams
were born, most of which you have made come
true. Or perhaps you did know. It was just about
midnight when you hooked your toes in the
anklets of your socks and pitched them across

the room, as though preparing to run through the dewy new grass. You have certainly been the finest and most perfect part of my life. But I sometimes wonder what you might have become without me, without me hanging around your neck in relentless poverty. Might you have become a rich woman? Without my constant suckling for approval and need for support, might you have found a creative avenue of your own?

And so here I sit, watching you sleep, exhausted from the day to day taking care of me instead of bursting exuberant into this new and important year of your life. Just don't remember me like this. Remember when I could haul fifty pounds of firewood into the house single-handed and lift you off the floor with one arm. No matter what happens, we have something that most people never do: the best. Happy Birthday. I love you forever.

ALEXIS DE VEAUX
Twilight

it is never a come suddenly.
abrupt as dawn: tearing the darkness
first illumination: erupting sleep
just below the skin of it.

never as visible
as skyline
as the woman on the bridge
nightly: electric. lapis.
not like her tai chi her
one leg pose
serene. against city: blue gray fog
lights.

here: take it, my friend
take this surrealian blue
mauve
cape of dusk. the last
before we embrace
a tongue behind the knee. suck on
the she sex of evening. take some
but take it
easy.

ALEXIS DE VEAUX

Cuntery

I will make a savannah of my
    dreads
I will make an incense of my
    pussy
I will make breadfruit of my
    hands
I will make a fetish for your
    love

MARILYN HACKER

From Cancer Winter

Should I tattoo my scar? What would it say?
It could say "K.J.'s Truck Stop" in plain English, highlighted with a nipple ring
(the French version: Chez K.J./Les Routiers).
I won't be wearing falsies, and one day
I'll bake my chest again at Juan-les-Pins,
round side and flat, gynandre/androgyne,
close by my love's warm flanks (though she's sun-shy
as I should be: it's a carcinogen

like smoked fish, caffeine, butterfat and wine).
O let me have my life and live it too!
She kissed my breasts, and now one breast she kissed
is dead meat, with its pickled blight on view.
She'll kiss the scar, and then the living breast.

○

I don't know how to die yet. Let me live!
Did Etty Hillesum think that, or Anne Frank,
or the forty-year-old schoolteacher the bank
robber took hostage when the cop guns swiv-
eled on them both, or the seropositive
nurse's aide, who, one long-gone payday, drank
too much, fucked whom? or the bag lady who stank
more than I wished as I came closer to give
my meager change? I say it, bargaining
with the *contras* in my blood, immune
system bombarded but on guard. Who's gone?
The bookseller who died at thirty-nine,
poet, at fifty-eight, friend, fifty-one,
friend, fifty-five. These numbers do not sing.

○

She'll kiss the scar, and then the living breast,
and then, again, from ribs to pit, the scar,
but only after I've flown back to her
out of the unforgiving Middle West
where my life's strange, and flat disinterest
greets strangers. At Les-Saintes-Maries-de-la-Mer,
lust pulsed between us, pulsed in the plum grove where
figs dropped to us like manna to the blessed.
O blight that ate my breast like worms in fruit,
be banished by the daily pesticide
that I ingest. Let me live to praise
her breathing body in my arms, our wide-
branched perennial love, from whose taproot
syllables shape around the lengthening days.

MAY SARTON
A Light Left On

In the evening we came back
Into our yellow room,
For a moment taken aback
To find the light left on,
Falling on silent flowers
Table, book, empty chair
While we had gone elsewhere,
Had been away for hours.

When we came home together
We found the inside weather.
All of our love unended
The quiet light demanded,
And we gave, in a look
At yellow walls and open book.
The deepest world we share
And do not talk about
But have to have, was there,
And by that light found out.

JUDITH MCDANIEL

From Body of Love

V.
Will I still wonder
at hummingbird wings
that vibrate into shadows
when she has become as familiar to me
as the tree that draws her?

Will I feel
the vibration in my heart
when your fingers flutter
down my spine

my quickening joy when you
open the door after being away

when this life together
is what we expect?

I want to know

if the hummingbird
who hovers over my head each morning
during breakfast on the patio
will still be a miracle to me in ten years.

if your body warm with sleep
pressed close against my back after
the alarm has rung and been turned off

if the sound of your laugh
deep and full

if the shape of your jaw

the scent of your

the curve. . .

MELANIE HOPE
Ashes

There's something nice about a teapot
Sharing quiet with you in the afternoon
I hate to think that one day
Someday this will end
That we have to swing into darkness
There are no songs for this yet

I want to sing you a song
Yes I want to sing you a song
I will use your vibrator
As my microphone
Serenade you
Standing above you in bed
I like the way I know
You would look at me then
I like the way I know you
Not too hot not too cold
Just right the way
I hover around your skin

Dusty trinkets on window sills
Wind chimes in unexpected places
I don't want to think of our ashes
Dark gray dust with flecks of bone
I would rather put on
My red crushed velvet dress
For my next song
A desperate Blues piece
For you I will croon
Until you come save me
From the state I'm in

Fireplaces with piles of wood
Red embers hissing to gray black ash
Too bad this will some day end

I don't want to go to wind
There will be no songs then
For me to sing or you to hear
There will be no you for me there

MARGARET RANDALL

I Am Loving You

FOR YOU, BARBARA

I am loving you in the furrowed temperature
of our bodies broadening soft
moving into the trust we fashion
this day and the next.
Holding each other, our children
becoming grandchildren, our grandchildren
growing into this world we want to change,
its broken law of greed and pain.

I am talking about the curve of a breast
in this time when nothing is given
and almost everyone dies before her time.
A trill of Sandhill cranes
hold captive breath and sky.
In some ancient cell I know our fingers
moved and touched, remembering.
Perhaps we were sisters, husband and wife,

perhaps we were mother and daughter
father and son, interchangeably.
In a future that requires
successful closure of the Salvadoran war,
all sides in the Middle East
to give something and get something,
I am loving you still
resting against your shoulder's heat.

I am loving you as the sun goes down in Matagalpa,
women like us stroking each other
in old high-ceilinged rooms, jacaranda patios
their walls pocked by the silent calibre
of old battles.
Sun rising over Johannesburg, over Belfast
pale through a narrow ravine on Hopi land
where a child pushes her flock before her
embracing herself against the wind.
Against the winds of change we shape the words
with our mouths that can say these things
because other women said them
and others dreamed them
looking then looking away
holding each other quickly, fear
standing at the door.

Pinatubo's* fallout
turns the evening clouds a burning red
above this New Mexico desert
where I am loving you now
long and carefully slow
with words like *wait* and *here* and *yes*
as we tell each other
the world is still a dangerous place.

We will take it one death at a time
claiming only the memory
of our trembling and our rage.

*Mount Pinatubo, in the Philippines, erupted most recently in 1991. The tremendous amount of volcanic ash spewed into the air traveled thousands of miles, reddening the sunsets in places as far away as New Mexico.

MELINDA GOODMAN
Love All The Time

Bald from the chemo
you decide the shape of your head
is comparable to Nefertiti's
striding proud in bright silks
from your carved mahogany doorway
to the hurricane battered blue Subaru
you drive your daily route to the mailbox
call to the man who guards the gate
"Good morning! Mail not come today yet?"
"Not yet!" he calls back, "Are you waiting for your love letters?"
"Yes," you say, laughing like sixty with sunlight
peaking behind your shades. "Yes, I'm waiting for my love letters."
"But Ms. L.," he says grinning, "You want love all the time."
"That's right!" you say shifting gears
peeling out   rolling his words on the palm of your tongue
like a piece of genuine St. Croix ginger hard candy
" 'Love all the time. . . .
Love all the time,' " you tell me
"Nothing wrong with that."

ADRIENNE RICH
Nights and Days

The stars will come out over and over
the hyacinths rise like flames
from the windswept turf down the middle of upper Broadway
where the desolate take the sun
the days will run together and stream into years
as the rivers freeze and burn
and I ask myself and you, which of our visions will claim us
which will we claim
how will we go on living
how will we touch, what will we know
what will we say to each other.

Pictures form and dissolve in my head:
we are walking in a city
you fled, came back to and come back to still
which I saw once through winter frost
years back, before I knew you,
before I knew myself.
We are walking streets you have by heart from childhood
streets you have graven and erased in dreams:
scrolled portals, trees, nineteenth-century statues.
We are holding hands so I can see
everything as you see it
I follow you into your dreams
your past, the places
none of us can explain to anyone.

We are standing in the wind
on an empty beach, the onslaught of the surf
tells me Point Reyes, or maybe some northern
Pacific shoreline neither of us has seen.
In its fine spectral mist our hair
is grey as the sea
someone who saw us far-off would say we were two old women
Norns, perhaps, or sisters of the spray
but our breasts are beginning to sing together
your eyes are on my mouth

I wake early in the morning
in a bed we have shared for years
lie watching your innocent, sacred sleep
as if for the first time.
We have been together so many nights and days
this day is not unusual.
I walk to an eastern window, pull up the blinds:
the city around us is still
on a clear October morning
wrapped in her indestructible light.

The stars will come out over and over
the hyacinths rise like flames
from the windswept turf down the middle of upper Broadway

where the desolate take the sun
the days will run together and stream into years
as the rivers freeze and burn
and I ask myself and you, which of our visions will claim us
which will we claim
how will we go on living
how will we touch, what will we know
what will we say to each other.

MURIEL RUKEYSER

Anemone

My eyes are closing, my eyes are opening.
You are looking into me with your waking look.

My mouth is closing, my mouth is opening.
You are waiting with your red promises.

My sex is closing, my sex is opening.
You are singing and offering : the way in.

My life is closing, my life is opening.
You are here.

ELOISE KLEIN HEALY

The Concepts Of Integrity And Closure In Poetry As I Believe They Relate To Sappho

1
There's always the question
what else? or *what more?*
A fragment of papyrus,

a frame from a film.
Wholeness but no closure.
Just what you'd glimpse—
two women suddenly arm in arm
crossing the beach-front walk,
the waves running like mares
behind them.

2
What is a month, for example?
Tear it out of a year like an eye
and what do you see?
Unimaginable to expect a year
could be missing an eye, or is it harder
to think of it
having one? Questions of parts
of what,
this is how I've felt
trying to look out of my self.
Just quick takes,
motor-driven and waiting for the day
it all makes sense.

3
Sappho is the lesson of parts.
Libraries you must do without
because you are the book.

4
This is what happens at parties
where women dance with one another.
Everyone kisses. Old lovers.
Tribes assume this.
Kiss and kiss. Just that much of that.
Book and book and book. I have been learned
by heart. Lovely Sappho taking in
a glance at a lovely thigh, flower
arranging someone's hair.
Like that.

Across the patio
in a canvas chair, you know
the living danger sitting there.
A fragmentary glance. An hour
in her arms, disarray
you carry for another hour
or a year, years from that day
you keep like a piece of mica or a negative.

I have held to my lips
for a moment things like smoke. Smoke
from a burning book.

5
The waves ran away like mares
and the silver sat in its soft cloth
and the shells of the sea rolled
and dragged lovingly up and back.
And some of those women simply saw
each other and some of them saw
the sea.

But Sappho, she saw everything.

RITA MAE BROWN
Sappho's Reply

My voice rings down through thousands of years
To coil around your body and give you strength,
You who have wept in direct sunlight,
Who have hungered in invisible chains,
Trembled to the cadence of my legacy:
An army of lovers shall not fail.

Magali Alabau  Becky Birtha

Paula Gunn Allen   Jacquie Bishop

Dorothy Allison   Beth Brant

Gloria Anzaldúa   Olga Broumas

Avotcja   Mi Ok Song Bruining

Robin Becker   Jane Chambers

BIOGRAPHIES

Magali Alabau was born in Cuba and settled in New York in 1966. Her first book of poems, *Electra, Clytemnestra*, was published in Spanish, followed by *The daily extreme unction (La extremaunción diaria, Sister (Hermana)*, and *Ilium (Hemos llegado a Ilion)*. *Electra, Clytemnestra* has been translated into English by Anne Twitty.

Paula Gunn Allen, M.F.A., Ph.D., Laguna Pueblo/Sioux (American Indian), is Professor of English at the University of California, Los Angeles. The mother of three children, she is a novelist, poet, and essayist of Native American myths and legends; she is also editor of *The Voice of the Turtle: American Indian Literature 1900–1970* and *The Song of the Turtle: American Indian Literature 1974–1994*.

Dorothy Allison's novel, *Bastard Out of Carolina*, a finalist for the 1992 National Book Award, has been translated into French, German, Greek, Spanish, Norse, and Italian. Her performance work, entitled *Two or Three Things I Know for Sure*, and a new novel, *Cavedweller*, are forthcoming. She lives in northern California with her partner, Alix Layman, and her three-year-old son, Wolf Michael.

Gloria Anzaldúa is a Chicana dyke-feminist, tejana patlache poet, writer, and cultural theorist from the Rio Grande Valley of south Texas now living in Santa Cruz. Her books include *Borderlands/La Frontera: The New Mestiza*, and the anthology, *Making Face, Making Soul/Haciendo Caras: Creative and Critical Perspectives by Feminists of Color*, which won the Lambda Literary Best Small Book Press Award.

Lanuola Asiasiga is a Samoan lesbian feminist, mother of three children. She was born in Aotearoa (New Zealand).

Avotcja is an activist, poet, radio broadcaster, musician, and photographer who lives and works in the Bay Area. At the forefront of many political and social struggles, she has a weekly radio show on KPFA-Radio Pacifica, where she created the Third World Department.

Robin Becker's fourth and newest collection of poems is entitled *Cross-Dressing for the Girls*. An associate professor of English at Pennsylvania State University, and a board member of the Associated Writing Programs, she serves as poetry editor for *The Women's Review of Books*.

Mary Bennett's two poems, "Cells" and "My Girlfriend," appeared in *A Gathering of Spirit: A Collection of North American Indian Women*, edited by Beth Brant. Her 1984 contributor note read: "(Seneca) I wrote these poems while in prison, serving time for possession of a dangerous weapon. Me and my girlfriend live in Chicago, happy to breathe polluted air. I'm fifty-three."

Becky Birtha is a Black lesbian feminist Quaker, mother of an adopted daughter, and happily in a new relationship. She has taught writing at Bryn Mawr. Her works include *The Forbidden Poems* and two short story collections, *For Nights Like This One: Stories of Loving Women* and *Lover's Choice*. She is currently writing stories for children.

Jacquie Bishop is a Black lesbian poet and feature writer living in her native Brooklyn. She is an AIDS, women's health-care, sex, and sexuality educator. Her work has appeared in a number of lesbian and gay presses. Her poetry manuscript is entitled *Thinking Out Loud.*

Beth Brant is a Bay of Quinte Mohawk from Tyendinaga Mohawk Territory in Ontario, Canada. She is editor of *A Gathering of Spirit,* writings and artwork by Native women. Her poetry, fiction, and essays include *Mohawk Trail, Food and Spirits,* and *Writing As Witness.* A grandmother, she lives with her partner of eighteen years, Denise Dorsz.

Olga Broumas, born in Syros, Greece, is poet-in-residence at Brandeis University. Her first book in English, *Beginning with O,* was a Yale Younger Poets selection. Her recent works include *Perpetua;* collaborative poems with T. Begley, *Sappho's Gymnasium;* and their book-length poem, *Helen Groves.*

Rita Mae Brown, poet, novelist, screenwriter, and teacher, wrote the now-classic lesbian novel *Rubyfruit Jungle.* Her work includes *Venus Envy, Starting from Scratch,* and *A Different Kind of Writer's Manual,* co-written with her cat, Sneaky Pie. She lives in Virginia.

Mi Ok Song Bruining is a Libran Rat, born in Korea, adopted in the United States. A social worker, poet, and artist, she is writing her first nonfiction book on international adoption issues.

Jane Chambers (1938–1983) is the author of twelve works written for the stage, including *Last Summer at Bluefish Cove;* one book of poetry, *Warrior at Rest;* two novels; as well as TV plays. Chambers was one of the very first writers to depict the love of woman for woman as an ordinary, nonspectacular way of being human.

Chrystos is of Menominee and Alsace-Lorraine/Lithuanian heritage. A self-educated artist and writer, she is an activist for Native rights and prisoners' causes. The author of *Not Vanishing, Dream On,* and *In Her I Am,* her forthcoming book is entitled *Fugitive Colors.* She lives in the Pacific Northwest.

Elizabeth Clare is a poet, essayist, and activist living in the Midwest, transplanted from the Pacific Northwest. She has an M.F.A. in Creative Writing from Goddard College. Her poems and essays have appeared in many publications including *Hanging Loose, The Disability Rag,* and *Sinister Wisdom.*

Cheryl Clarke is an African-American lesbian-feminist poet. Her four books are: *Narratives: Poems in the Tradition of Black Women, Living as a Lesbian, Humid Pitch,* and *experimental love.* An editor of *Conditions, 1981–1990,* she is director of The Office of Diverse Community Affairs and Lesbian-Gay Concerns, Rutgers University.

Michelle Cliff is Allan K. Smith Professor of English Language and Literature at Trinity College. She is the author of the novels *Abeng, No Telephone To Heaven,* and *Free Enterprise;* a collection of short fiction, *Bodies of Water;* and *The Land of Look Behind,* a book of prose and poetry.

Jo Whitehorse Cochran has an M.F.A. in Creative Writing from the University of Washington. Her work has appeared in many publications, including *Changing Our Power: Introduction to Women's Studies* and the revised edition of *Lesbian Studies.* She lives in Seattle with her cats, Bob, Romaine, and Wind Willow.

Almitra David won the Eighth Mountain Press Poetry Prize for *Between the Sea and Home*. In addition to her chapbook, *Building the Cathedral,* her poems and translations have appeared in many journals. She teaches Spanish at the Friends Select School in Philadelphia.

Barbara Deming (1917–1984) is known today primarily for her courageous political work and writings related to civil rights, feminist causes, and peace. Her love poems reveal the private side of her passionate involvement with the world. Her writings are newly available in *Prisons That Could Not Hold,* edited by Skye Vanderlinde.

Alexis De Veaux is a poet, playwright, novelist, and author of *Don't Explain, A Song of Billie Holiday*. Formerly poetry editor for *Essence* magazine, she is on the faculty in the Department of American Studies at the State University of New York at Buffalo. Her children's books include *Na-Ni, An Enchanted Hair Tale,* and the forthcoming *Woolu Hat.*

Rachel Guido deVries is a poet and novelist who lives in Cazenovia, New York. Her collection of poems is entitled *How to Sing to a Dago.*

Ana Bantigue Fajardo came to the United States from the island of Luzon in the Philippines at the age of four. *Lolo* Pete, her paternal grandfather, a fisherman, is an ancestor guide who continues to inspire her. A graduate student at the University of California in Santa Cruz, she is studying indigenous communities in the Philippines.

Jan Freeman is the award-winning author of *Hyena* and *Autumn Sequence.* Her poems and essays have appeared in *The Oxford Anthology of Women Poets in the United States* and *The Key to Everything*. She is a contributing editor for *The American Poetry Review* and lives in western Massachusetts.

Suzanne Gardinier was born in New Bedford, grew up in Scituate, Massachusetts, and first kissed a woman after a lacrosse match in a college locker room in Madison, New Jersey. She is the author of *The New World,* teaches at Sarah Lawrence College, and lives in Brooklyn.

Beatrix Gates, author of *Native Tongue* and *Shooting at Night,* appears in the anthologies *The Key to Everything* and *Gay and Lesbian Poetry in Our Time*. She is collaborating on an opera, *The Singing Bridge*. Founder of Granite Press, she serves on the Kitchen Table: Women of Color Press Transition Team.

Elena Georgiou is currently a graduate student in the creative writing program at City College, City University of New York, in New York City.

Gabrielle Glancy has published widely. She lives in San Francisco.

Alvia G. Golden "came late to writing, but got lucky." At the age of forty-eight, she was accepted into Audre Lorde's writing program at New York's Ninety-second Street Y. She then studied at Sarah Lawrence College with Jean Valentine, Jane Cooper, Grace Paley, and Tom Lux, among others. Her book of short stories is entitled *Acts of Love.*

Jewelle Gomez, activist and writer, was born in Boston, and lived in New York City for twenty-two years. The author of *Oral Tradition: poems old and new,* and a book of essays, *Forty Three Septembers,* she is adapting her novel, *The Gilda Stories,* for performance with the Urban Bush Women Dance Company. She lives in San Francisco, where she teaches creative writing and popular culture.

Melinda Goodman teaches poetry workshops at Hunter College in New York City. Her self-published collection of poems is called *Middle Sister.* Her latest manuscript is entitled *Suck My Heart.* Goodman was a 1991 winner of the Astraea Lesbian Poets Award.

Janice Gould is a California native of Koyangk'auwi Maidu and European descent. The author of *Beneath My Heart,* she is in the English doctoral program at the University of New Mexico in Albuquerque.

E. J. Graff's fiction and essays have appeared in *The Iowa Review, The Kenyon Review, Ms., The New York Times, Out, The Women's Review of Books,* and a variety of anthologies. She was a 1993 winner of an Astraea National Lesbian Action Foundation's Emerging Writers Award.

Judy Grahn's many books of poetry and prose include the groundbreaking gay and lesbian cultural history *Another Mother Tongue.* Her latest book is *Blood, Bread, and Roses: How Menstruation Created the World.* She teaches at the California Institute for Integral Studies.

Marilyn Hacker is the author of eight books, most recently *Winter Numbers* and *Selected Poems 1965–1990.* She received a Lambda Literary Award in 1991 for *Going Back to the River* and the National Book Award in 1975 for *Presentation Piece.*

Eloise Klein Healy is a poet and teacher whose work includes *Building Some Changes, A Packet Beating Like a Heart,* and *Ordinary Wisdom.* Her most recent collection, *Artemis In Echo Park,* was nominated for a Lambda Book Award and is available on CD and audiotape (The Women's Studies Chronicle, New Alliance records). She teaches at Antioch University in Los Angeles.

Georgia Heard is a poet, artist, and teacher who travels around the country speaking about poetry. She lives in New York City.

Melanie Hope is a tomboy turned lesbian poet who lives in New York City. Her ancestors came to the United States from Nevis and Guyana.

Maya Islas, born in Cuba, has resided in the United States since 1965. She has an M.A. in Psychology. Author of *Sola, Desnuda, Sin Nombre, Sombras-Papel, Altazora,* and *Merla,* she is the recipient of the 1993 Latino Literature Prize in Poetry. She works at the New School of Social Research in New York City.

Gale Jackson is a poet, writer, storyteller, librarian, educator, and student of history. She is currently on the faculty of Medgar Evers College, City University of New York. Her poetry manuscript is entitled *Conversations with Love.*

Melanie Kaye/Kantrowitz is the author of *We Speak In Code: Poems and Other Writings; My Jewish Face and Other Stories;* and *The Issue Is Power: Essays on Women, Jews, Violence, and Resistance.* The former editor of *Sinister Wisdom,* and executive director of Jews for Racial and Economic Justice in New York City, she also teaches women's studies and writing.

Chrystos

 Rachel Guido deVries

Elizabeth Clare

 Ana Bantigue Fajardo

Cheryl Clarke

 Jan Freeman

Almitra David

 Suzanne Gardinier

Barbara Deming

 Beatrix Gates

Alexis De Veaux

 Elena Georgiou

Gabrielle Glancy   Marilyn Hacker

Alvia G. Golden   Eloise Klein Healy

Jewelle Gomez   Georgia Heard

Melinda Goodman   Melanie Hope

Janice Gould   Maya Islas

Judy Grahn   Melanie Kaye/Kantrowitz

Irena Klepfisz is the author of *A Few Words in the Mother Tongue: Poems Selected and New* and a companion volume *Dreams of an Insomniac: Jewish Feminist Essays, Speeches and Diatribes*. An activist in the lesbian/women/Jewish communities, she is editorial consultant on Yiddish language and culture for the North American Jewish feminist magazine *Bridges*.

Jacqueline Lapidus is an editor and theologian whose poems and essays have appeared in many feminist periodicals and anthologies. Her books of poetry include *Ready to Survive, Starting Over,* and *Ultimate Conspiracy*. She shuttles between Provincetown and Boston.

Joan Larkin has published two collections of poetry, *Housework* and *A Long Sound*. She coedited the first anthology of lesbian poetry, *Amazon Poetry*, and later anthologies *Lesbian Poetry* and *Gay and Lesbian Poetry In Our Time*. Her play is entitled *The AIDS Passion*. She teaches in the Goddard College M.F.A. program in creative writing and lives and writes in New York City.

Lê Thi Diem Thúy is a writer and performer. Born in South Vietnam, she was raised in southern California. Some of her work appears in *The Very Inside: An Anthology of Writing by Asian and Pacific Islander Lesbian and Bisexual Women,* edited by Sharon Lim-Hing.

Audre Lorde (1934–1992) introduced herself as "Black, Lesbian, Poet, Mother, Warrior Woman." Pioneering poet and international activist, her ten volumes of poetry and five of prose include *Zami: A Biomythography, The Marvelous Arithmetics of Distance: Poems 1987–1992,* and *The Cancer Journals*. Cofounder of Kitchen Table: Women of Color Press, she was New York State Poet Laureate (1991–1993).

Elizabeth Lorde-Rollins, M.D., is a Black physician, a resident in Obstetrics and Gynecology at Columbia-Presbyterian Medical Center. After graduating from Harvard University in Psychology, she taught third grade at P.S. 46 in New York City. Awarded her M.D. from Columbia's School of Physicians and Surgeons, her research interests include acupuncture in obstetrics.

Victoria Lena Manyarrows is a Tsalagi/Eastern Cherokee lesbian active in community arts, education, health, and social programs in the Bay Area. She has a Masters in Social Work and is the recipient of an Astraea National Lesbian Action Foundation's Emerging Writers Award. Her essays and poems have been widely published. *Songs from Native Lands* is her first full-length book.

Judith McDaniel lives in Tucson, Arizona, where she writes and teaches writing and communications courses. Her most recent publication is *A Lesbian Couples Guide*. Other books include the novels *Winter Passage* and *Just Say Yes,* and several collections of poems and essays. She has recently completed *Taking Risks,* a collection of poetry.

Mary Ann McFadden has written four collections of poetry since 1973. The second, *Eye of the Blackbird,* was chosen for the Writer's Voice First Book Reading Award in 1991. Her poems have appeared recently in *The American Voice, Southern Poetry Review,* and *Kestrel*.

Honor Moore's most recent book, *The White Blackbird,* is a biography of her grand-mother, the painter Margarett Sargent. *Memoir* (poetry) appeared in 1988. She lives in Connecticut and is completing a new book of poems.

Cherríe Moraga, a native of Los Angeles, now lives in San Francisco. She is coeditor of *This Bridge Called My Back* (The Before Columbus Foundation American Book Award Winner) and author of *Loving in the War Years*. She is also a playwright whose work has been widely performed.

Robin Morgan, political theorist and feminist activist, is an award-winning poet who has published five books of poetry and ten of prose, including the groundbreaking *Sisterhood Is Powerful*. Her most recent book of poems is *Upstairs in the Garden: Selected and New Poems*. A founder of The Sisterhood Is Global Institute and former editor-in-chief of *Ms.*, she lives in New York City.

Mardy Murphy has an M.F.A. in creative writing. She was the editor and publisher of *Squeezebox* Magazine/Paper Tigress Press, and *Equal Times,* the first feminist newspaper in the Midwest during the 1970s. She is an independent management and public relations consultant in northern California.

Eileen Myles is a poet and performer who conducted an openly female presidential campaign in 1992. Her books include *Chelsea Girls* (Lammy Award); a collection of short stories, *Not Me;* and *Maxfield Parrish/early and new poems*. She is coeditor of *The New Fuck You: Adventures in Lesbian Reading*.

Pat Parker (1944–1989), Black lesbian poet, political activist, and coalition builder, broke many silences on intimate woman-to-woman dynamics. Her work includes *Womanslaughter, Jonestown and Other Madness,* and *Movement in Black: The Collected Poetry of Pat Parker 1961–1978*. Mother of two daughters, softball player, she was the director of the Oakland Feminist Women's Health Center.

Michelle Parkerson is a writer/filmmaker based in Washington, D.C.

Gerry Gomez Pearlberg's writings have appeared in *Calyx, Global City Review, Women on Women 3,* and *Sister and Brother: Lesbians and Gay Men Write About Their Lives Together*. She edited *The Key to Everything* and *The Zenith of Desire*. She lives in Brooklyn with her boxer Otto, to whom she has written many love poems. She also goes for girls.

Minnie Bruce Pratt's second book of poetry, *Crime Against Nature,* the 1989 Lamont Poetry Selection chosen by the Academy of American Poets, was nominated for a Pulitzer Prize. Her books include *We Say We Love Each Other, Rebellion: Essays 1980–1991,* and *S/He,* stories about gender boundary crossing. Her new work is a series of narrative poems, *Walking Back Up Depot Street*.

Margaret Randall's most recent books are *Gathering Rage: The Failure of Twentieth Century Revolutions to Develop a Feminist Agenda, Sandino's Daughters Revisited,* and *Our Voices/Our Lives: Stories of Women from Central America and the Caribbean*. She is working on a book about women and money and writing poems that double as recipes. She lives in New Mexico.

Naomi Replansky was born in the Bronx in 1918. Her first book, *Ring Song,* was published by Scribner in 1952 and was nominated for the National Book Award. A collection of her work is available in *The Dangerous World: New and Selected Poems 1934–1994*.

Bessy Reyna was born in Cuba and raised in Panama. In 1990, she received an individ-

Irena Klepfisz  Judith McDaniel

Jacqueline Lapidus   Mary Ann McFadden

Joan Larkin  Honor Moore

Audre Lorde   Cherríe Moraga

Elizabeth Lorde-Rollins, M.D.   Robin Morgan

Victoria Lena Manyarrows   Mardy Murphy

Eileen Myles

 Naomi Replansky

Pat Parker

 Bessy Reyna

Michelle Parkerson

 Adrienne Rich

Gerry Gomez Pearlberg

 Margaret Robison

Minnie Bruce Pratt

Karla E. Rosales

Margaret Randall

Kate Rushin

ual artist's award from the Connecticut Commission on the Arts. Her work has appeared in many anthologies, most recently in *In Other Words: Latina Writers in the U.S.*

Adrienne Rich has published fourteen books of poetry, the most recent of which is *The Dark Fields of the Republic*. Her three prose books include the classic feminist work *Of Woman Born: Motherhood As Experience and Institution*. Recipient of the Academy of American Poets' fellowship and the John D. and Catherine T. MacArthur fellowship, she lives in California.

Margaret Robison was paralyzed on her left side by a stroke at age fifty-four. She now leads creative writing workshops for women with disabilities. Her books are *The Naked Bear* and *Red Creek*. Her work has been published in such journals as *Sojourner, Disability Rag, Sinister Wisdom, Negative Capability,* and *Yankee Magazine*.

Karla E. Rosales is an out Latina lesbian spoken-word artist, educator, consultant, and community organizer. Her work has been published and presented locally and nationally. She lives on the West Coast.

Muriel Rukeyser (1913–1980) published eighteen volumes of poetry, beginning with *Theory of Flight*, which won the Yale Younger Poets Award in 1935. One of this century's most esteemed poets, *The Collected Poems* reflects her passionate personal journey, a life of love and politics, justice and human rights. Newly available is *Out of Silence: Selected Poems* and *A Muriel Rukeyser Reader*.

Kate Rushin is an African-American poet and teacher. Her first book of poems, *The Black Back-Ups*, was nominated for a Lambda Book Award. Awarded the Grolier Poetry Prize in 1988, her work has appeared in numerous journals and anthologies. She is director of The Center for African American Studies, and is Visiting Writer at Wesleyan University in Connecticut.

Barbara Ruth wrote the poem reprinted here, "The Politics of Relationships," twenty years ago. She says, "I am softer now, less solid, still yearning for freedom. Daughter of Yemaya, student of the dharma, my occupations include cultivating a beginner's mind, practicing revolutionary love, and, in all my contradictions, living the question."

Sappho (c. 612–558 B.C.) was a celebrated lyric poet of Greece whose work was burned c. A.D. 380 by early Christians in Constantinople and again in the eleventh century at the time of Pope Gregory VII. The extant fragments of her songs are considered masterpieces. Her home on the island of Lesbos became a women's colony dedicated to Aphrodite and the arts.

May Sarton (1912–1995), born in Belgium and a longtime resident of New England, lived her later years in Maine. Her first published poems at age seventeen launched a career that includes fifty-four volumes of poetry, novels, journals, essays, and children's books. Recent publications are *From May Sarton's Well*, with photographs by Edith Royce Schade, and *Collected Poems 1930–1993*.

Susan Sherman is a poet, playwright, essayist, and editor of *Ikon* magazine, whose most recent book is *The Color of the Heart: Writing from Struggle and Change 1951–1990*. She has received a New York Foundation for the Arts poetry fellowship and a Puffin Foundation Grant for her memoir-in-progress, *Amerika's Child*.

Barbara Ruth   Pamela Sneed

Susan Sherman   Kim Vaeth

Ana Sisnett   Lisa Vice

Anita Skeen   Fran Winant

Linda Smukler  Merle Woo

Ana Sisnett is a Black immigrant worker, parent, and budding genealogist. A human rights and computer networking/electronic media activist, she is affiliated with several progressive organizations and women of color locally, nationally, and internationally.

Anita Skeen grew up outside of Big Chimney, West Virginia, where she brought dogs into her house, books into the woods, and filled her childhood with an assortment of girls who were interested in everything from Davey Crockett to paper dolls to basketball. Author of *Each Hand a Map*, she is professor of English at Michigan State University in East Lansing, where she teaches creative writing and women's studies.

Linda Smukler is the author of *Normal Sex*. She has won awards in poetry from the New York Foundation for the Arts and the Astraea Lesbian Writers Fund. Her work has appeared in numerous journals and anthologies.

Pamela Sneed is a New York City–based Black Lesbian poet, activist, actor, performer. She has toured internationally, written and performed three solo performance works to date, and is completing a volume of poems for publication.

Gertrude Stein (1874–1946), born in Pennsylvania, chose to live in Paris where she and Alice B. Toklas were central figures in the cultural life of the interwar years. In an innovative and controversial style, she wrote poetry, novels, plays, opera libretti, and nine volumes of prose. For beginners, see Judy Grahn's *Really Reading Gertrude Stein: A Selected Anthology with Essays*.

May Swenson (1913–1989) received many honors for her eleven volumes of poetry, including *Another Animal* and *In Other Words*. Recent collections are *The Love Poems of May Swenson* and *Nature: Poems Old and New*. Awarded a John D. and Catherine T. MacArthur Fellowship, she was a chancellor of the Academy of American Poets.

Kim Vaeth's three recent small-press publications each were nominated for the Pushcart Prize, including *Her Yes*. A finalist in the 1989 Massachusetts Artists Fellowship Program in poetry, her poems have appeared in *Calyx, The Women's Review of Books, Ploughshares, The American Voice, 13th Moon*, and *The Kenyon Review*. She teaches writing at Simmons College in Boston.

Lisa Vice's newly published first novel is entitled *Reckless Driver*. She lives in Carmel Valley, California, with her partner, writer Martha Clark Cummings.

Fran Winant's poems have appeared in anthologies including *The Penguin Book of Homosexual Verse*, and were performed by Ian McKellen on Broadway and at the Gay Games. Her painting is discussed in *The Sexual Perspective*, by Emmanuel Cooper. Her self-published books of poems are available from Violet Press, P.O. Box 398, New York, NY 10009. She has just completed her first novel.

Merle Woo is a socialist feminist educator, writer, and is active in Radical Women and the Freedom Socialist Party. She teaches women's studies at San Francisco State University.

PERMISSIONS

237

CREDITS FOR
PHOTOGRAPHS OF CONTRIBUTORS

Paula Gunn Allen: courtesy of Melinda Fay; Dorothy Allison: courtesy of Jill Posener; Gloria Anzaldúa: courtesy of Margaret Randall; Robin Becker: copyright by Miriam Goodman; Jacquie Bishop: courtesy of Pat O'Brien; Beth Brant: copyright 1991 by Tee Corinne; Olga Broumas: copyright by Ariel Jones; Mi Ok Song Bruining: copyright 1995 by Yuki Tung; Jane Chambers: courtesy of Beth Allen; Chrystos: courtesy of Ana R. Kissed; Cheryl Clarke: courtesy of George Ganges; Barbara Deming: courtesy of Judith McDaniel; Alexis De Veaux: courtesy of Jonathan Snow; Rachel Guido deVries: courtesy of Jan Phillips; Suzanne Gardinier: copyright by Star Black; Beatrix Gates: copyright by Becket Logan; Jewelle Gomez: courtesy of Val Wilmer; Melinda Goodman: courtesy of Gina Rhodes; Janice Gould: courtesy of Margaret Randall; Judy Grahn: courtesy of Jean Weisinger; Marilyn Hacker: copyright 1987 by Robert Giard; Eloise Klein Healy: courtesy of Sheree Rose; Melanie Kaye/Kantrowitz: courtesy of Sarah Bolden; Irena Klepfisz: courtesy of Linda Eber; Joan Larkin: courtesy of Diane Edington; Audre Lorde: courtesy of Dagmar Schultz; Victoria Lena Manyarrows: copyright 1992 by Teresa Scherzer; Judith McDaniel: courtesy of Tee A. Corinne; Honor Moore: courtesy of Robert Giard; Cherríe Moraga: copyright 1993 by Jean Weisinger; Robin Morgan: courtesy of Sally Tagg; Pat Parker: courtesy of Marilyn Humphries; Michelle Parkerson: courtesy of Leigh H. Mosley; Gerry Gomez Pearlberg and Otto: courtesy of Carmelita Tropicana; Minnie Bruce Pratt: courtesy of Doug Lawson; Margaret Randall: courtesy of Marvin Collins; Naomi Replansky: courtesy of Charles Lewis; Bessy Reyna: courtesy of Pit Pinegan; Adrienne Rich: courtesy of Gypsy P. Ray; Margaret Robison: courtesy of Pat Bega; Kate Rushin: courtesy of Marilyn Humphries; Susan Sherman: copyright 1991 by Colleen McKay; Linda Smukler: copyright by Becket Logan; Kim Vaeth: copyright 1993 by Craig Bailey; Lisa Vice: copyright 1994 by Robin Rosenzweig; Merle Woo: copyright by Phyllis Christopher. All other photographs are courtesy of the contributors.